# set-apart motherhood

## REFLECTING **JOY** AND **BEAUTY**
## IN FAMILY LIFE

*Leslie Ludy*

**NAVPRESS**

*A NavPress resource published in alliance
with Tyndale House Publishers, Inc.*

NavPress is the publishing ministry of The Navigators, an international Christian organization and leader in personal spiritual development. NavPress is committed to helping people grow spiritually and enjoy lives of meaning and hope through personal and group resources that are biblically rooted, culturally relevant, and highly practical.

A NavPress resource published in alliance with Tyndale House Publishers, Inc.

*NAVPRESS* and the NAVPRESS logo are registered trademarks of NavPress. Absence of ® in connection with marks of NavPress or other parties does not indicate an absence of registration of those marks.

*TYNDALE* is a registered trademark of Tyndale House Publishers, Inc.

ISBN 978-1-61291-676-7

Cover design by Annie Wesche
Cover photo by istockphoto.com

Some of the anecdotal illustrations in this book are true to life and are included with the permission of the persons involved. All other illustrations are composites of real situations, and any resemblance to people living or dead is coincidental.

Some of this material has been previously published at setapartgirl.com and in *Set Apart Girl* magazine.

Cataloging-in-Publication Data is Available.

Printed in the United States of America

| 20 | 19 | 18 | 17 | 16 | 15 | 14 |
|----|----|----|----|----|----|----|
| 7  | 6  | 5  | 4  | 3  | 2  | 1  |

Of all the various titles I've held, none mean more than wife, mom, and Mimi to our twenty grandchildren. I'm grateful that God blessed Dennis and me with six souls to guide, shape, and point to Him. Leslie expertly does the same for the reader, guiding us to Him who controls all as we face the challenges and trials on this journey called motherhood.

**BARBARA RAINEY**
wife of Dennis Rainey, author, artist, and creator of Ever Thine Home

Moms don't need more frilly advice. They need real wisdom. Fortunately Leslie delivers this and so much more in *Set-Apart Motherhood*. She doesn't talk from a stuffy sofa in a professionally designed studio. She speaks from the heart of a woman who is dealing with soured milk in her van and spaghetti sauce on her carpet. Now *this* is a woman I want to listen to! Leslie has an art for bringing joy and peace to the most chaotic career in the world—motherhood.

**HANNAH KEELEY**
TV host, *Hannah, Help Me!*
Founder, Mom Mastery University

# TABLE OF CONTENTS

# PART ONE

# A VISION FOR SET-APART MOTHERHOOD

*Heavenly Perspective for the Sacred Call of Mothering*

# CHAPTER ONE

# THE SACRED CALL OF SET-APART MOTHERHOOD

*Gaining God's Perspective on Raising Kids*

*Strength and honor are her clothing;*
*She shall rejoice in time to come.*

PROVERBS 31:25

I AM A *REAL* MOM. My days are filled with moments that are oh-so-real-life, not to mention unglamorous and unromantic. Like the other day, when my youngest daughter threw up all over her car seat just as church was getting out. So right there on the sidewalk while everyone was walking past in their dress pants and high heels, my husband and I went through the tedious and rather embarrassing process of cleaning up the mess while trying to keep our kids' behavior in check as they ran wildly around the church lawn. We made quite a spectacle. We were an hour late for our family outing. Our kids were whining about being hungry and complaining about the smell in the car. And everyone was just a little on edge, including Mommy. But once we finally got to our destination and ate lunch in the warm sunshine, it turned out to be a meaningful day being together as a family. It just took a little bit of battling to get to the beauty.

That's the way motherhood is for me. Battling through the daily challenges of mothering to discover the incredible beauty God has waiting for me on the other side. I have learned not to stop short and accept chaos as the norm, or resign myself to the attitude, "Motherhood will always be messy and frustrating." By God's grace, I have purposed not to settle for anything less than *His* pattern for motherhood—and His pattern is victorious, joy-filled, and beautiful.

I have been around countless moms who roll their eyes at the notion that motherhood can be beautiful. They laugh at the idea that there can be dignity in raising children. They scoff at the suggestion that a mom of small kids can be calm, well-groomed, and well-rested. They snicker at the idea that a home with young children can be clean, beautiful, and orderly.

Believe me, I understand where these sentiments come from. I understand how challenging it can be to experience beauty, order, and dignity in the midst of mothering little ones. Eric and I were married for nearly ten years before we had children. Then God in His providence (and divine sense of humor) blessed us with four kids in four years (via two adoptions and two biological children). Since we'd been in public ministry for most of our married life, we thought we were seasoned at handling challenges. But the pressures of speaking in front of large crowds, meeting book deadlines, and leading a global ministry pale in comparison to the pressures of parenting four children. Three of our kids were in diapers at the same time, and the youngest two had only seven months between them due to an adoption and surprise pregnancy that happened simultaneously. Though we had a wonderful support system of people who helped us keep an orderly home during that season, there were still many moments of diaper blowouts, baby spit-up on the carpet, ear-splitting tantrums, chaos, and constant commotion . . . not unlike that scene from *How the Grinch Stole Christmas*, when the Whos down in Whoville are making all their "Noise! Noise! Noise!"

Now that my kids are a bit older (eight, six, five, and four at the time of writing this book), things are a little less chaotic in our home, and we have gotten past the diaper blowouts, for which I am thankful. But the noise level is about the same, as are the constant demands of raising four young children so close in age. My days are not filled with picturesque Pottery Barn Kids moments but with noisy, messy, and often extremely exasperating scenarios.

Case in point: Last week I spilled about half of a container of milk on the floor of our van. I don't remember all the details of how it happened, but my guess is that I was unloading kids and groceries at the same time. As usual, I was attempting to carry way more than was humanly possible, while simultaneously mediating a squabble between my two youngest kids and trying to get my six-year-old to stop decorating her white shirt with the pink sidewalk chalk she'd discovered on her way into the house. Consequently I spilled a large amount of milk all over the carpeted van floor. Which resulted in the smell of sour milk permeating our vehicle. Which resulted in kids whining and complaining about the smell every time they got in the car. Which resulted in me loading up all the kids the next morning and driving thirty minutes to the only car wash I knew that could shampoo car floor mats.

I unloaded four rowdy kids into the car wash parking lot, removed all of the car seats, and stashed all the random toys, books, and miscellaneous items into a duffle bag so the van would be clear for its thorough cleaning and the floor mats for a good washing. I hauled the kids, the car seats, and the duffle bag up the crowded sidewalk into the waiting area and got ready to pay for the car wash, making sure to mention that I wanted the carpets shampooed.

The sleepy college-aged guy at the counter then informed me that they had decided to stop doing carpet shampoos for the rest of the day, so all I could get would be the basic wash and vacuum. I'm not sure why they chose to stop shampooing carpets the moment I arrived, but I was convinced that they had made the decision for the express purpose of making my life more difficult.

"I just drove thirty minutes to have you shampoo the carpets," I protested. "Isn't there anything you can do to help me?"

"Well," he said in a distinctly nonhelpful tone, "why don't you just come back tomorrow?"

*Uh . . . come back tomorrow? Excuse me, buddy. You really don't understand my life. I'm a mom of four little kids! It's a huge ordeal to load them up and take an hour out of my day to get the van carpets shampooed. Don't you get it? I can't come back tomorrow. Tomorrow I have to take one kid to the doctor, another to speech lessons, and another to buy new tennis shoes because his current ones are so caked with mud that they have morphed from light blue to dark brown. I also have to fold five loads of laundry, or my kids will be going to school in their pajamas. And I have to go back to the grocery store because I forgot to buy paper towels. Not sure when I'm going to fit that in. My schedule is super full. I can't even tell you all the things on my to-do list! There's no way I can just drop everything and come back tomorrow to have you shampoo my van carpets, okay?*

Those were pretty much my exact thoughts, and I'm glad I did not voice them out loud. A perfectionist by nature, I like it when things flow smoothly. I am not a fan of inefficiency, such as multiple trips to the car wash in a twenty-four-hour period to clean up milk that should never have been spilled in the first place. But with kids, things don't always go like clockwork. All my carefully laid plans have a way of growing wings and flying out the window. When that happens, life as a mom can feel stressful and frustrating.

But once I got home and the kids and I went outside into the crisp fall air, we ended up having a fun afternoon building memories together. Somehow during those next few days, the van carpet got cleaned, the new tennis shoes got purchased, most of the laundry got done, and (shockingly) we managed to survive for a while without paper towels. The saga of the spilled milk was soon forgotten, and it turned out to be a beautiful week full of great family milestones and memories, such as our youngest son finally learning to ride his bike without training wheels.

Motherhood is not easy and never will be. But I have discovered that motherhood can be marked by beauty, joy, and incredible fulfillment when I focus on Jesus Christ, instead of on all the inconveniences and struggles I face along the way.

## RISING ABOVE MEDIOCRITY

"Life with kids is chaos," a mother of four once told me. "We might as well get used to it!"

"My kids have destroyed all semblance of order in my life. I can't even remember what my house looks like clean or what it feels like to get a good night's sleep," a harried mother of three complained to me.

These are common thoughts among today's moms. And I know from personal experience how tempting it can be to throw up our hands and jump on the "motherhood is chaos" bandwagon.

Mothering can be intensely frustrating and often feels futile. Being a mom disrupts every aspect of your life. Mothers have no downtime, no vacation from raising kids. We cannot take a break from our calling as mothers. It's a job that requires us to be on call twenty-four hours a day, seven days a week. There is little private time. (Many mornings when I take a shower, my four- and five-year-old stand outside the bathroom banging on the door and yelling for me to hurry up). And moms of small kids can't just clean the house every few days and expect it to stay that way. We have a team of little rascals working to *undo* all of our hard work around the house. They play with the laundry we just folded and dump all our makeup out of the drawer we just organized. They spill spaghetti sauce on freshly cleaned carpet and draw with marker on newly painted walls. Alas, I know these scenarios all too well.

In moments such as these, the voice of Despair whispers to my soul, *Your life is so chaotic. You might as well give up on expecting anything more. Don't even try. It's always going to be this way.*

Then the voice of Self-Pity chimes in: *Poor, poor you. No one understands how hard your life is. Raising four little kids is so stressful and difficult. Everyone else has it so easy, but you never get a break!*

My response to these voices is what leads to either victory or defeat in my mothering. If I entertain these lies, even for a moment, they take root in my soul and grow. Soon the whole day becomes chaotic and discouraging. I feel overwhelmed and exhausted, and my efforts to bring order and peace seem futile. The moment I resign myself to the "life with kids is chaos" attitude, I no longer have the energy to battle for beauty, order, and peace. I'm resigned to mediocrity.

But when I cry out to God for victory, He comes to my

rescue. He gives me the strength to resist the temptation to throw my hands up in despair or wallow in self-pity. He redeems a day that might otherwise have ended in discouragement and fills it with peace and joy. He calms my tumultuous emotions. He quiets my hyper children. He helps me find their missing shoes. He gives me wisdom for how to organize our routine so that leaving the house becomes smoother and easier. And He opens my eyes to see the sacred privilege He's given me—helping shape, nurture, and train four future world-changers.

God intends for mothers to experience amazing delight and fulfillment in raising children and running a home. That doesn't mean that raw and real-life moments won't happen or that every day will end like an episode of *Little House on the Prairie*. It simply means that when God is at the center of our mothering, there is beauty, order, peace, joy, honor, and dignity to be found, by His grace.

I don't believe mothers of young children are destined to constantly have peanut-butter handprints all over their walls and piles of dirty laundry all over the floor. I don't believe it is a mother's lot to wear sweats every day and never have time to put on makeup or dress with dignity. I don't believe moms have to be slaves to their children's emotional tirades and temper tantrums or wallow in exhaustion and despair. Though I have succumbed to each of these scenarios more than once over the past few years, I believe that God has something so much more for my motherhood than defeat and mediocrity.

Proverbs 31 describes what a set-apart mother looks like. She is an active and busy mom. But even with all the responsibilities she carries, she is not frenzied, frazzled, or frumpy. "Strength and dignity are her clothing," and "she smiles at the future" and "looks well to the ways of her household" (Prov. 31:25,27, NASB). She dresses with beauty and dignity, provides for the needs of her household, seeks high-quality materials, and works eagerly with her hands to create beauty, order, peace, and security for those under her care. The Bible makes it clear that God's pattern for godly motherhood leads to beauty, joy, dignity, honor, and strength. And this pattern is available to each of us when we submit every aspect of our motherhood to Him.

God desires to take an ordinary mom and transform her into a radiant, set-apart, "joyful mother of children" (Ps. 113:9). What an exciting promise!

I've never met a mother who feels like she's doing everything perfectly. And that is a relief, because neither do I! We must always remember that being a good mother doesn't mean being perfect. It means becoming dependent upon the only One who is. Whenever I lean fully and completely on Jesus Christ, He faithfully points me to *His* perfect pattern for motherhood, one situation at a time.

At its essence, set-apart motherhood is not about trying to impress people with our parenting skills but about humbly applying God's Truth to every challenge we face as mothers. Set-apart motherhood means diligently seeking to become the mothers God has called us to be, one step at a time.

Our job is not to try to become supermoms or Proverbs 31 women in our own strength. Our job is to surrender to God without reserve and to trust Him with every detail of this heavenly calling. No matter how ill-equipped you may feel as a mother, God has a beautiful purpose for your motherhood role, and He desires you to be strong and prepared for this sacred task.

Remember, faithful is He who calls you, who also will do it (see 1 Thess. 5:24)!

## LET'S TALK ABOUT IT

*Group Study and Discussion*

1. **Read Proverbs 31:10-31.** Why do many women struggle to believe that this picture of godly motherhood is possible in today's world? What makes it possible to live out this calling?

2. **Read Philippians 4:4 and 1 Thessalonians 5:16.** Have you ever seen a mother who embraces her calling with consistent joy? What did you notice about her attitude and the way she interacts with her kids? Is this an attitude that all mothers can have? How?

3. **Read Hebrews 12:1.** What does it mean to rise above mediocrity in our mothering? Where do we gain the strength to do so?

## TAKE IT DEEPER

*Personal Study and Reflection*

**Read:** Proverbs 31:25-27

**Reflect:** Does this picture of motherhood seem unrealistic? If so, why? Do I believe that God desires to bring joy, beauty, and dignity to my motherhood role? Am I willing to pursue and expect this?


**Read:** 1 Thessalonians 5:16-18

**Reflect:** How do I typically respond to stresses in mother-hood—with thanksgiving and joy, or with despair and self-pity? In which areas is God asking me to adopt a heavenly perspective toward my role as a mother?


**Read:** 1 Thessalonians 5:24

**Reflect:** What does it mean to rely on God's grace to become the kind of mother He has called me to be, rather than pursuing "parenting perfection"?

# CHAPTER TWO

# MOTHERING WITH JOY

*Viewing Motherhood Through Heaven's Eyes*

*He grants the barren woman a home, like a joyful mother of children.*

PSALM 113:9

FOR MOST OF MY LIFE, I've been an expert multitasker. My motto is, "Why do only one thing when you could get three things done at once?" or "Why put it off until later when you could get it done right now?" Over the years, this approach has led to a highly productive life, with many accomplishments and neatly checked-off task lists under my belt.

But my productivity has decreased exponentially with each new child God has given me. Any mother on the planet could tell you that efficiency and young children simply do not mix. My children have the uncanny ability to destroy, in less than five minutes, a room that took me an hour to clean. My oldest son frequently "reorganizes" storage spaces around the house just for fun, forcing me to spend large amounts of time later undoing his creative damage. And all too often, I accomplish only one of the five things I had planned to do with my kids on a given day, because one of them starts whining, another decides to pester his siblings, and two more begin squabbling over a toy, requiring me to spend my morning getting everyone's attitudes back on track. My six-year-old has been known to take a full half hour to eat three bites of toast. My youngest son is so easily distracted while brushing his teeth that the task almost always takes ten minutes instead of two. And why is it that whenever I take extra time to dress up the kids for an event, at least two of them end up with ink spots, toothpaste stains, or spilled food all over their fancy clothes?

Even though I'm wired to be productive and efficient, being a mother has forced me to use the majority of my time and energy on tasks that seem mundane and unimpressive, such as scraping dried toothpaste from the bathroom countertop or searching the house from top to bottom for a precious stuffed animal that has gone MIA.

Amy Carmichael, a missionary to India in the early 1900s, wrote about being required to make a choice between traveling, speaking, and doing "big things" for the kingdom of God or taking care of many small children in need of love and guidance. As she was wrestling with this decision, she and those who worked alongside her in ministry called to mind the scene when Jesus willingly humbled Himself and washed His disciples' feet.

"*He took a towel*—the Lord of Glory did that," Amy wrote. "Is it the bondservant's business to say which work is large and which is small, which unimportant and which worth doing? . . . Children tie the mother's feet, the Tamils say. . . . We knew we could not be too careful of our children's earliest years. So we let our feet be tied for love of Him whose feet were pierced."[1]

"Children tie the mother's feet." That statement describes my life quite well. The more children God blesses me with, the less productive and more restricted my life becomes.

Motherhood has hampered my knack for getting things done and greatly diminished my personal freedom. Even going to the grocery store has become a luxury that must be carefully strategized. I can't hop in my car and run to the mall or coffee shop whenever the mood strikes. (In fact, I don't even remember what that feels like!) "Alone time" doesn't happen unless I get up well before the break of dawn. In order to accomplish a project like cleaning out my closet or painting a bedroom, I have to plan it about a month in advance so that I can line up child care.

Gone are the highly effective workweeks in which I systematically checked off every item on my task list and ended each day with a clear inventory of accomplishments. These days, I might spend an entire morning teaching Avonlea how to roll Play-Doh into a ball, setting up a treasure hunt in the backyard for Hudson, dancing to the *Mickey Mouse Clubhouse* theme song with Kipling (I sing this in my sleep now), and examining a ladybug with Harper. I spend countless hours every week picking up rooms that become messy again within hours, repeating instructions over and over again until I feel like a broken record, and reading stories like *The Little Red Hen* or *Knuffle Bunny*.

Yes, my current life is less productive, less exciting, and less globally influential than my former life. But is it less important?

No.

In fact, the opposite is true. As Amy Carmichael wrote, "The Master never wastes the servant's time."[2]

Productivity is not God's highest goal for this season of my life; obedience is. Success in His kingdom is not measured by accomplishments or accolades. Rather, God says, "Whoever desires to become great among you, let him be your servant," (Mt. 20:26) and "Whoever gives one of these little ones a cup of cold water in the name of a disciple, assuredly, I say to you, he shall by no means lose his reward" (Mt. 10:42).

As I take the "lower place" of spending my best time, energy, and talents on my children, I am serving the One who gave His life for me, the One who left His home in heaven in order to wrap a towel around His waist, humble Himself, and tenderly wash my dirty feet.

Whenever I start to view motherhood as mundane, unimpressive, and unexciting, I must remember that it is my great privilege to "allow my feet to be tied" for the love of Him whose feet were pierced.

## THE PURPOSE OF MOTHERHOOD

Many women today view parenthood as a way to enhance their lives and bring them happiness. Moms-to-be dream of showing off their children in adorable Baby Gap outfits and decorating the nursery with all the latest trends on Pinterest. We are eager for the fun and exciting parts of motherhood, but rarely are we prepared for the incredible sacrifice of motherhood. And when raising kids turns out to be far more demanding, messy, and time-consuming than we bargained for, we are tempted to become discontent and disillusioned.

In his powerful sermon "Ten Shekels and a Shirt," Paris Reidhead stated, "It's not what you're going to get out of God. It's what He's going to get out of you."[3] Likewise, motherhood should not be about what we are going to get out of it but about what God is going to get out of it. Motherhood should be something we do for His glory, not our own selfish whims and desires.

God gets glory out of our motherhood when we selflessly love and serve the children He has entrusted to us even when parenting is difficult. We honor Him in our mothering when we willingly embrace the challenging task of leading our little ones to Him. He blesses us with children not merely for our own personal satisfaction but so that we can raise them up for His kingdom.

Yes, children can and do bring great happiness and enhancement into our lives. But if these things are our primary reasons for becoming mothers, we are missing the purpose of motherhood.

When I evaluate my role as a mom solely on what enjoyment and benefit it is bringing me, I quickly lose my joy and become frustrated by the tedious task of training my children in godly behavior, the exhausting job of nursing sick kids through sleepless nights, and the shocking lack of personal time that mothering offers. But when I approach motherhood for the sole purpose of bringing glory to God, I find tremendous joy in making personal sacrifices for my children. As I seek to honor Him in my motherhood, it becomes my delight to give my best to my children, without concern for what I'm getting out of it, but only with what He is getting out of it.

Walking out my motherhood in the grace of God and doing each task wholeheartedly, out of love and obedience to Him, is the secret to mothering with joy (see Col. 3:23). It's not a happiness that depends upon the cleanliness of my house or the behavior of my kids; it's an abiding contentment and peace, no matter what challenges I'm facing.

I certainly haven't mastered the art of abiding in that state of "motherhood joy" twenty-four hours a day. But by His grace, I'm learning more and more how to delight in loving and serving my children as an act of love unto my King.

## BEING "ALL THERE"

Jim Elliot wrote, "Wherever you are, be all there."[4]

Never have I been more challenged in applying this

principle than with my four young children. It's so easy to be with them physically, yet disengaged from them mentally and emotionally. When you spend countless hours conversing with preschoolers and toddlers, it's easy to feel brain-dead and look for a way to tune out. For the past few years, my conversations with my children have centered around things like animal noises, ("Mama, what does a camel say?" "Um, I'm not exactly sure, buddy. . . . Let's talk about what a cow says!"), reminders about the purpose of food ("Eat your eggs please, and don't throw them at your brother!"), and discussions about proper social behavior ("We don't hit others in the head with our squishy toy lizard, Harper.")

It can be mind-numbing at times. I often find myself wanting to "escape"—just to tune out the squawks, screams, and childish chatter and pay attention to something else for a little while, something more intellectually stimulating. It's easy to tell my children to "go play" while I indulge in an enjoyable activity of my own, like calling a friend, checking e-mail, or surfing the Internet for new recipes or decorating ideas. None of those pastimes are wrong in themselves, but God has made it clear where my focus is to be when I'm with my children—on them.

Proverbs 31:27 says, "She watches over the ways of her household, and does not eat the bread of idleness." And Titus 2:5 exhorts mothers to be "homemakers." When God tells us to watch over the ways of our households, He means a constant vigilance, a never-ending watchfulness, like a soldier guarding a castle. There is no allowance for idleness or "let's just go brain-dead" moments.

When I take my kids to the park, I have two choices: I can either find another mom to chat with and ignore my kids as they run around burning off their excess energy, or I can engage with my children—play with them, laugh with them, help them on the swings and slides, and give my complete attention to their playtime. This takes energy that I sometimes don't feel like I have. Yet when I ask God for the grace to give my best to my children, He is always ready and able to give it.

The souls of my children hang in the balance.

If I "unplug" and tune them out, I leave my children open and vulnerable for the Enemy to gain access into their lives. It might be the cruel words of another child at the park. Am I paying attention and ready to protect my child from destructive taunts or worldly influences? Or am I off in another world, chatting away with another mom or checking e-mail on my phone? It might be a behavior pattern in one of my kids that is not honoring to God. Am I willing to tackle it with the best of my energy? Or do I simply pretend not to notice it because it takes too much stamina to apply truth to the situation and train my child to do what is right?

God says I'm not to give one moment of my day to idleness, not to check out mentally and emotionally when I'm with my kids. Rather, I am to maximize every moment with my children and continually point them to truth.

The other morning after spending four hours of focused time with my kids, I was relieved to have a little window of time to get some things done while the younger kids were resting and the older kids were playing. But as soon as I sat down to check my e-mail, Hudson burst into the room, asking how to spell five different words for a book he was writing. Harper followed close on his heels, begging me to make a princess crown for her precious Lambie (a well-loved, well-worn stuffed lamb she has had since infancy) out of colored pipe cleaners. Sigh.

I thought of Martha, who was "distracted with much serving" (Lk. 10:40) and overlooking the more important activity that Mary had chosen. I relate to Martha far more than I'd like to admit. How easy it is to give in to the urgent tasks and disregard the important ones! There were two precious children, creating, inventing, playing, and exploring. And they were inviting me to share their childlike delight of discovery. Making a princess crown for Lambie and helping Hudson with his new literary release were of far more eternal value than checking my e-mail. But to do so required a choice of self-denial—saying no to what I wanted to do (take a break!) and saying yes to the opportunity before me (showing enthusiasm for my children's world).

God has called me to motherhood, with all of its interruptions, inconveniences, and intensities. If I lean upon His grace and not on my own strength, He gives me the ability to go the extra mile, even when I do not feel like it. Whether it is being diligent to train my children instead of letting certain behaviors slide, getting up early so I am prepared for my teaching time with the kids, or saying no to various "self outlets" during the day, I have found unexpected joy in being "all there" for my kids.

This is not an easy commitment. When we choose not to "eat the bread of idleness," there is very little free time and very little "me" time, but the rewards of such devotion and obedience are eternal. As it says in Proverbs 22:6, "Train up a child in the way he should go, and when he is old he will not depart from it."

It takes focus, dedication, and energy to train children in the way they should go. And though motherhood is the most taxing job we will ever undertake, it also has the potential of being the most joyful and most rewarding task we could ever imagine . . . if we do it for the glory of our King.

We can't be partially committed to this call; we must give it everything we have.

## LET'S TALK ABOUT IT

### Group Study and Discussion

1. **Read Matthew 10:42 and 20:26.** How should the principle of taking the "lowest place" affect our calling as mothers? How does God want us to respond when raising children decreases our productivity or efficiency?

2. **Read Colossians 3:23.** What does it mean to approach our motherhood for the glory of God and not our own personal benefit? How does this lead to joy in our mothering?

3. **Read Proverbs 31:27 and Titus 2:5.** Do you know a mother who consistently gives her best focus and energy to her children? What do you notice in her life as a result of this attitude?

## TAKE IT DEEPER

*Personal Study and Reflection*

**Read:** Psalm 113:9

**Reflect:** Do I believe that it is God's desire for me to find consistent joy in my motherhood role? Are there specific areas of motherhood that God is asking me to approach with a heavenly perspective instead of a selfish one? If so, which areas?

**Read:** 1 Corinthians 10:31

**Reflect:** Have I been approaching motherhood out of joyful obedience to God or simply for my own personal benefit? Are there any sacrifices God is asking me to make in order to make His glory the primary goal of my mothering?

**Read:** 2 Timothy 2:4 and Colossians 3:23

**Reflect:** What does it mean to "be all there" when I'm with my children? Are there any changes I need to make in my daily life in order to follow this principle? How will these changes impact my children and home life?

# PART TWO

# SET-APART MOTHERHOOD
# MADE PRACTICAL

*Inspiration and Ideas to Help Each Day Flow Smoothly*

CHAPTER THREE

# GETTING BEYOND THE FRAZZLE

*Choosing Peace over Chaos*

*I can do all things through Christ who strengthens me.*

PHILIPPIANS 4:13

ONE TIME WHEN my youngest son, Kipling, was about three, I was driving down the highway when suddenly he began hollering from the backseat. I glanced into my rearview mirror and saw that both he and his car seat had somehow toppled sideways. Kip was leaning on his side and staring out the window with wide eyes and a horrified expression. While he was not in any immediate danger, he was terrified. It was about three minutes before I was able to pull off to the side of the road safely and straighten things out. During those three minutes, though I tried to reassure him that he would be okay, he kept yelling, "Mama! I can't handle it! I just can't handle it!" Kip sounded (and looked) so hilarious that I couldn't help but laugh, though I did feel bad for the poor little guy. His world had taken an unexpected turn, and he did not know how to deal with the sudden stress.

I can relate to that feeling. As a mother of young children, there are many moments when I am tempted to proclaim, "I can't handle it! I just can't handle it!" Like those nights when—after a crazy, nonstop, exhausting day—my husband and I finally get the children all tucked into bed and are just sitting down in the living room to enjoy some peace and quiet, only to be called back downstairs about twenty times to mediate sibling squabbles, refill sippy cups with water, and tuck in comforters that have somehow, in the space of five minutes, managed to become loose and "uncozy." Or the time a few months ago when one child spilled red paint all over his clothes, another had an accident on the hardwood floor, and still another threw up on the new carpet, all in a one-hour stretch of time.

At least five or six times every day—usually in my busiest moments—four needy little people simultaneously call out, "Mamma?!" and demand my attention, oblivious that my hands are full already. If my nerves are already on edge, it can feel like a mob of wild monkeys closing in around me. Those are the moments when my emotions begin to scream, "I can't handle it!" or "I just want to clean up the kitchen in peace!"

Other times, when I'm feeling especially spent, I start wistfully envisioning myself lounging on a beach with a good book instead of sweeping crushed Cheerios off the floor for the umpteenth time.

Recently I took my youngest daughter, Avonlea (also known as Avy) to our local "open gym" for preschoolers. When we arrived, the gym was packed with rambunctious three- and four-year-olds and their parents. Then I realized—it was spring break. None of the preschools in the area were in session, and some of the day cares were closed as well.

Oblivious to the crowd, Avy happily jumped on the trampoline and catapulted into the foam pit. But I couldn't help noticing how tired and depressed most of the other moms seemed. A week of no school had taken its toll on them, and now their little ones were running around out of control as the mothers sat and zoned out or vented to their friends about how difficult their children were and how chaotic their lives felt.

"I can't wait until nap time comes today," one mom said to her friend. "I'm going to make them sleep for three hours while I collapse on the couch in front of a movie."

There have been plenty of times when I've had similar feelings. Usually it happens when life is busier than normal and our routine gets interrupted, or when Eric and I are distracted by a major challenge in our ministry. Suddenly the children's behavior goes south, the house looks like a tornado hit it, and I feel like I've just been in a train wreck.

The other night was one of those times. Eric had been out of town for three days, and I was playing the role of single mom. The weather had been strangely snowy and cold despite the calendar saying it was spring. The kids were cooped up in the house, whiny and bored, and missing Daddy. I was in the middle of a huge organizing project, which meant that there were piles all over the house that kept getting bigger as the kids dug through them looking for "treasures." The house was getting messier and messier, and the kids didn't seem to be able to play for more than five minutes without a meltdown.

I've learned that those "I can't handle it" or "I'm exhausted" moments present great opportunities for victory in my mothering.

Not victory in my own strength but in the strength of Jesus Christ. In my weakness, His strength can be made perfect. But I must allow that supernatural work of grace to be accomplished in my soul by trusting Him for strength and peace, instead of giving in to how I am feeling in the moment.

"I can't handle it" feelings must immediately be countered with a "God *can* handle it" attitude. Without God's supernatural grace and strength, I would quickly become an exhausted, stressed-out, emotional mom yelling at my children all day long and constantly looking for ways to escape my responsibilities at home. But when I lean upon the grace of God, everything changes. I am learning how to handle stressful parenting situations according to God's pattern and not my own.

Instead of focusing on how exhausted I feel, which then causes me to feel sorry for myself, lash out in frustration, or throw my hands up in defeat and allow chaos to reign, I can ask for God's help, knowing that with Him all things are possible (see Mt. 19:26). He and He alone can grant me the grace to handle, with strength and dignity, any and every parenting challenge that comes my way. By God's grace, mothering can be victorious and triumphant, despite the constant demands and complications that our children bring into our lives, when we lean on His strength and not our own.

## MAKING IT PRACTICAL

I'd like to share some practical steps and principles that I have found to be helpful in replacing motherhood frazzle and exhaustion with the perfect peace of God:

### 1. CHOOSE THE RIGHT KIND OF "ME TIME"

All moms need a periodic reprieve from the nonstop intensity of mothering. But it is all too easy to turn this need for a break into an outlet for selfishness. We put our home and family life into a tailspin when we ignore our children and household tasks while spending hours talking or texting with girlfriends, browsing Pinterest, posting on Facebook, or shopping. These activities are not necessarily wrong in themselves, but they must be put into proper balance. When we look to these things as a way of "escape" from taking care of our home or our family, we are putting "me time" in an unhealthy position in our lives.

Certainly there is nothing wrong with spending time alone to refuel and recharge. Reading a good book, journaling, taking a long walk, or having an encouraging chat with a trusted friend can be wonderful ways to gain perspective. But it's important not to give in to the voice that whispers,

*You should really take a break from serving your family. They demand too much of you. You need to take time for* you*!* The decision to take time to refresh and refuel should flow from a motive of becoming stronger and more equipped to serve your family, not from self-pity or resentment.

I have found that the best "me time" is actually not "me time" at all but "God time." Prayer, journaling, worship, and reading Christian biographies refreshes my soul far more than vegging in front of a movie, browsing Pinterest, or going on a shopping spree.

Remember, our relationship with Christ is meant to be the "anchor of the soul" (Heb. 6:19). If we allow it to fade into the background, our perspective will be out of whack. But when we put Him first, everything else in life falls beautifully into place (see Mt. 6:33). So do whatever it takes to spend time in His presence each day. If you have to, get up earlier, sneak away to a quiet place while your kids nap, forgo Facebook time (I know . . . gasp!), or even turn on a movie for your little ones (an edifying one, of course!).

If you are feeling depressed or overwhelmed, remember that running *to* Him, not *away* from Him, is the solution. His Word says, "The LORD is near to those who have a broken heart, and saves such as have a contrite spirit" (Ps. 34:18). When your emotions take a downward spiral, don't turn to Facebook, Twitter, television, shopping, or venting to your friends as your primary means of finding peace. Instead, run to the "God of all comfort" (2 Cor. 1:3).

When I say no to personal indulgences in order to say

yes to time in the presence of God, I discover that I'm not missing out on anything. I find all the lasting joy, peace, and strength I need in Him. Psalm 16:11 says, "In Your presence is fullness of joy." May we allow that reality to be proven true in our lives, instead of turning to the empty allurements of the world.

## 2. MEDITATE ON TRUTH

When life takes a hectic turn or when my emotions begin to protest against the constant demands of my children, a simple meditation on God's reality can turn everything around. Whenever my emotions are screaming the opposite message, I often remind myself of this verse: "I can do all things through Christ who strengthens me" (Phil. 4:13). When I dwell upon this remarkable promise, I realize that I have no excuse to whine, complain, or give in to the "I can't handle it" feelings. With God's strength, I can rise up like an athlete and run that extra mile. When He strengthens me, I *can* handle it, even when my emotions say otherwise.

One of the ways I keep God's Truth in the forefront of my mind is listening to audio Scripture on my iPhone: when I'm driving in my car, when I'm getting ready in the morning, and when I'm cleaning up the house. Hearing God's Word spoken has a way of grounding me in Truth. It takes my eyes off myself and places them on Christ. I hear His words of wisdom, guidance, comfort, and peace throughout the day, and it is hard to be frazzled when thoughts of His Truth fill my mind. Isaiah 26:3 says, "You will keep him in perfect peace, whose mind is stayed on You." Meditating on Scripture keeps our minds fixed upon Jesus, which leads to perfect peace.

Listening to worship music is another great way to keep Truth alive and fresh in my daily life. Edifying music brightens my perspective and sets a peaceful tone in our home. When my preschoolers are busy singing along to worship songs, they forget about the toy that they are squabbling over, or that one of them just stepped on the other one's pinky finger. Likewise, when I'm listening to music that helps me focus on Jesus, that pile of dishes in the sink or the mess on the playroom floor doesn't feel quite so overwhelming, because I'm focused on Him and not my circumstances.

### 3. RECRUIT SOME HELP

Often we mothers are convinced we must do everything alone. But when we take that one-woman-show attitude into our parenting, we miss out on the beauty of working together with our spouses and with the body of Christ. Dads are often far more willing to help out than moms realize. Usually they just need to be asked for help—in a clear, calm, nonaccusing way.

Approaching your husband with the attitude, *Get off the couch and come help me, why don't you!?* probably will not garner much positive response. But if you appeal to him in a loving, respectful way, he will most likely respond well. Eric is one of the most helpful husbands around; however, he needs clear direction on what must be done in the moment. If I say, "Could you please get the kids ready for bed?" he has a hard time knowing what needs to be done. But if I say, "Would you mind putting the kids into their pj's and helping them brush their teeth?" it gives him a clearer focus. I usually go so far as to lay the pj's out for him, because for most husbands (mine included), the task of searching through a child's closet to find the right clothing in the right size can be completely overwhelming!

If your husband is unable to help (or if he is out of the picture completely), consider approaching others in your life who may be able to step in and lend a helping hand. Most of us have parents, neighbors, or friends who would be happy to offer assistance in areas where we feel overwhelmed. Do not be afraid to ask for help (in a reasonable way, of course).

This does not mean turning your children over to someone else to raise so you can live a life of ease and leisure. But swapping babysitting with a trusted friend (you watch her kids one afternoon a week, then she watches yours the next week), sharing a cooking day with your mom or sister, or hiring a young woman from church to help you with laundry are all simple things that can make a world of difference to a harried mom.

Even with Eric's help around the house, I still have a rotation of wonderful young women who provide support to me in areas such as laundry and food preparation. As Christian mothers, we have a strong and supportive community in the body of Christ. If we can swallow our pride and ask for help where help is needed, it goes a long way to combat the frazzle of busy motherhood.

## 4. CLEAN THE KITCHEN

Years ago I read an article by a wife and mother about how she was able to write a novel from home. I don't remember most of the article, except for one point she made: "For an immediate sense of order and control, clean the kitchen thoroughly." Her advice sounded almost too simple, and yet I have found the principle to be true. When life feels frenzied and out of control, I can transform my perspective by taking time to clean the kitchen, make the beds, and declutter the house. When my house is clean and in order, I find new strength to face whatever situation I am dealing with. But when the house is cluttered and disorganized, every challenge seems about ten times larger than it really is.

Even if you feel that you don't have time to clean everything, just setting the timer for fifteen minutes and blitzing through the house to straighten things up can make a world of difference. And while you are at it, play some uplifting worship music or audio Scripture, which will help to change your perspective even more!

(Note: We will cover this principle in greater detail in chapter 4: Creating a Sanctuary.)

## 5. GET MOVING

When I am run-down or emotionally exhausted, the last thing I want to do is get outside and take a brisk walk or an invigorating bike ride. However, I have learned that exercise clears the mind and refreshes the body. When I feel apathetic, I must not listen to the voice of Self-Pity. You know, the one that whispers, *You poor thing; you have had such a hard time lately. You deserve to stay in bed!* or, *You should take it easy, you know. Lie on the couch and watch movies all day. You are too depressed and tired to do anything else!*

Taking that bait can be deadly to a mother's soul and toxic to a family's environment. It's certainly important for moms to get adequate sleep and even to nap during the day if needed. However, when kids see their mom constantly lying around, worn out and unhappy, they feel insecure. Our husbands and children need us to be active, involved, energetic, and available. Remember, God has called us to be "keepers of our homes." He will give us the grace to live out that calling if we call on Him for help.

Of course, there may be seasons when spending extended time in bed is necessary, such as during illness, pregnancy, or postpartum difficulties. But if you are simply experiencing the everyday fatigue that comes with mothering young children, you'll likely find energy you never knew you had simply by building more exercise into your day.

So if you are struggling with "mommy exhaustion," get out of bed, get off the couch, and move! Get some uplifting worship music in your headphones, put your little ones in the double stroller, and take a brisk walk outside, or go for a bike ride with your kids and enjoy God's amazing creation. A game of tag with your kids is a great way to get exercise and build memories at the same time. If the weather is not good, find ways to get moving indoors. Put on some upbeat music and dance with your kids, or take twenty minutes while they are napping to jump on the treadmill or do some stretching. On the days when I discipline myself to exercise, my emotions are far more stable and calm than on the days when I don't make time for it. Exercise (when done for God's glory and not self-glory) can be a wonderful pick-me-up for a tired mom!

## 6. DRESS WITH DIGNITY

It disturbs me when homemakers look like slobs, using the justification, "Why should I bother looking nice? I'm just hanging out with kids all day long." If a mom only makes herself look nice when she goes out to meet other people, she sends the message to her husband and kids that they are not as worthy of her efforts as other people are. This attitude disregards the value of guiding a home and caring for a family, and it shows a lack of sensitivity to those closest to her.

I've observed that when a mother dresses with dignity, she takes her role far more seriously, and the work she is doing begins to actually feel valuable and important. There is a big difference in how I feel on days when I've dressed hurriedly in sweats than on days when I put effort into my appearance. When I am dressed sloppily, I am more prone to feel lethargic and unmotivated as I go about my daily tasks. But when I dress with dignity, I'm reminded that this job deserves my best attention and focus. Most of us wouldn't show up for an office job dressed in sweats. So why should we dress haphazardly for our work in the home?

Of course there are certainly exceptions to this principle.

On days when I am cleaning out the garage or baking with the kids, it's just more practical to wear jeans and a sweatshirt. But on most days, I am more effective and focused in my mothering when I dress with dignity. It reminds me that my calling as a mother is worthy of my very best effort and that my family is deserving of honor and respect.

When we don't put any effort into how we look, we tend to feel depressed and defeated as we go about our daily tasks. But when we dress purposefully for our job as keepers of our homes, it reminds us of the importance of what we are called to and helps bring energy and dignity to our motherhood role.

This doesn't mean that you need to mop your kitchen floor in a formal dress and high heels. But even if you are going to be home all day, take a few extra minutes to "beautify" in the morning—whether it's layering a colorful cardigan over a casual shirt, adding some curl to your hair, or putting on some lipstick and a bit of fun jewelry. Just taking a few simple steps to dress with dignity can do wonders for your outlook and energy level.

## 7. DIG DOWN DEEP

As mothers, we all have moments when it is easier just to sit down on the couch (or plop in front of the computer) instead of doing the tasks sitting in front of us. If my preschooler starts whining or negotiating for a privilege, it's a lot easier for me to give in to his whim, rather than take extra time to train him how to ask properly. When my daughters are arguing over a toy, the easiest solution is to give each of them an iPad and tell them to go into separate rooms and play some learning games or watch a *Veggie Tales* episode. It takes a lot more effort and "umph" on my part to stop and help them resolve the conflict and make things right with each other. I would much rather take fifteen minutes to clean up the kids' playroom myself, rather than exert time and energy to engage my children in the process of tidying up.

But I have found that if I discipline myself to "dig down deep" and give extra energy to the things I do not feel like doing, I am less prone to exhaustion and defeat in the long run. That's because when we moms habitually cut corners in our parenting, it leads to much bigger and more challenging, time-consuming, and emotionally exhausting issues, such as children who never learn how to share toys, clean up their messes, or properly ask for things! Next time you want to cut corners, ask God for the strength to dig down deep and go the extra mile. The success and breakthroughs you experience will give you newfound energy and morale in your motherhood.

✳ ✳ ✳

There are a lot of times when I flip open a Pottery Barn Kids catalog and think, *If only my house and family looked like that, I would never feel burned-out or exhausted!* Many days I wish that our bedding could always stay that crisp, our playroom could always stay that organized, and my kids' attitudes could always stay that happy and content.

But no matter how perfectly my kids may behave, how

adorably their rooms may be decorated, or how smoothly my daily routine may flow, those things don't provide lasting joy, peace, or supernatural grace and energy. Only Jesus Christ can offer the strength we need to give our very best to our kids for the long haul.

The next time you sense that train-wreck feeling approaching, run to the One who can turn your exhaustion into exhilaration. He alone can transform any defeat into a glorious victory.

Remember, God has called you to be a joyful mother of children, not a frazzled, frenzied one. And whatever He calls us to, He equips us for. So do not buy the lie that motherhood is chaos. Choose to embrace God's pattern for parenting and rely on His supernatural strength alone, and you will find that He will carry you through each day on "wings like eagles" (Is. 40:31).

## LET'S TALK ABOUT IT

*Group Study and Discussion*

1. **Read Mark 1:35 and 6:46.** During Jesus' earthly ministry, where did He go to find refreshment and strength? How can we learn from His example when we feel run-down and in need of refueling?

2. **Read Philippians 4:13.** Have you ever observed a mother who was able to handle great challenges by relying on God's strength? What did you notice about her life?

3. **Read Psalm 113:9 and Isaiah 26:3.** Why do so many mothers today feel frazzled and frenzied? What is God's solution for mothering with joy and peace?

## TAKE IT DEEPER

*Personal Study and Reflection*

**Read:** John 15:4-5

**Reflect:** In what areas of my motherhood might God be challenging me to lean on His strength instead of my own willpower? How can this impact my perspective toward motherhood?

**Read:** Proverbs 31:27

**Reflect:** Are there areas in my mothering where God is asking me to "dig down deep" and give my best instead of cutting corners?

**Read:** Isaiah 40:31

**Reflect:** Do I believe that God can lift me above exhaustion and defeat? Are there any practical changes I should make in my daily life that can help me find new strength in Him?

*Answer: All very good!*

# CHAPTER FOUR

# CREATING A SANCTUARY

*Building Your Home into a Haven of Peace*

*Let all things be done decently and in order.*

I CORINTHIANS 14:40

WHEN ERIC AND I were first married, we visited the home of a Christian family with many young children. The father picked us up from our speaking event in their minivan. As we slid into the backseat, I had to move several crumpled McDonald's Happy Meal boxes off the seat to make room for us. When I buckled the seat belt, a sticky jam-like substance transferred onto my hand. Eric reached behind him and pulled out a small, plastic robot that had been jabbing him in the back. Toys, crayons, and bits of chips and crackers littered the floor.

The father smiled apologetically. "Sorry about the mess," he said. "But we have five kids. You'll understand when you have a family. It's impossible to keep anything clean. We never even bother to pick up this van anymore; it just gets trashed again the next day!"

The family's home was also a disaster. We had to watch our every step in order to avoid crushing the dolls, trucks, games, and books scattered all over the living room. The five young children careened about the house, yelling, shrieking, and laughing. Dishes, cookbooks, and junk mail cluttered the kitchen countertops. The bathroom looked like it had not been cleaned in months.

At dinner, the couple told us about their strong conviction that the primary way Christians could evangelize the world was by having a large family. But I kept wondering what kind of testimony the disorder in their lives was giving the outside world. The mother attempted to give me some advice to tuck away for the future. "Having children changes your life, honey. You have to get used to your house always being in disarray. That's just the way it is with kids."

I'd always wanted to be a mother, but this experience and others made me wonder if I wanted to have kids after all. I met one mom after the next who told me that a chaotic lifestyle and disorderly home environment were to be expected once I had kids. Their sour comments began to defuse my enthusiasm for having a family. Was it true that children removed all dignity, order, and cleanliness from a woman's life and surroundings? Sure, I'd grown up with a mom who kept a beautiful, clean, and orderly home. But our family only had three children. Were these women right? Was it impossible for a large family to have order? Or maybe my mom was the exception to the rule. I wasn't sure what to think, but the more frazzled moms and messy homes I observed, the more hesitant I became about having lots of kids, or even having kids at all.

A few years later, my perspective changed. I read a powerful book that showed me what was possible when a woman yields every aspect of her home, family, and motherhood to Jesus Christ. The book chronicled the lives of many great Christian women such as Elizabeth Fry, Catherine Booth, and Sarah Edwards: women who had large families, and world-changing ministries—and managed both with grace, excellence, and dignity. Their homes were clean and well ordered. They were feminine and dignified in their appearance. They made an eternal impact on the world around them. They showcased biblical motherhood. Their children and husbands respected and praised them (see Prov. 31:28).

Seeing these women's lives expanded my vision. It brought dignity back to the idea of mothering. I began to allow God's Word, rather than the experience of so many worn-out moms, to shape my perspective when it came to raising children and managing a home. As I studied Scripture and Christian women throughout history, I gained a clear, exciting picture of what my home and family life could be.

As mentioned earlier, I am very familiar with the overwhelming challenge of trying to keep order in a home with so many little hands working overtime to mess things up and the temptation to accept chaos and disorder as the norm. But, by the grace of God, I have learned that our home environment does not need to be the constant disaster that others prophesied it would be. In fact, as I have turned to Scripture, it's become clear to me that God's plan for motherhood is not just having children and raising them well but also being "keepers of our homes"—creating and maintaining a beautiful and orderly environment in which family life can thrive.

It doesn't require a PhD to recognize that children who grow up in an orderly, peaceful environment will be far more secure, calm, and happy than those who grow up in chaos. God is a God of peace and order, and when our homes reflect His nature, our families thrive.

However, this doesn't mean that we should be consumed with keeping our living rooms photo-ready for the cover of *Better Homes and Gardens*. In fact, women who become obsessed with their homes being perfect all the time create just as much stress for their families as those who accept chaos and disarray.

As we strive to maintain order and peace in our homes, we must remember that the *spiritual state* in our homes is far more important than their physical condition. If my heart is not right before God, then no amount of organizing or cleaning will create a peaceful home atmosphere. The cleanliness and order of my home should be an outflow of the cleanliness and order of my soul, or it will be meaningless and ineffective. Nor should keeping an orderly home flow out of a desire to impress other people with my decorating and organizational skills. It should flow out of a desire to serve my husband and children by creating an environment that facilitates stability and peace and reduces confusion and stress. It is an act of love.

God has given us the opportunity of building our homes into sanctuaries that cater to His priorities: intimacy with

Christ, hospitality, and family closeness. None of these can be accomplished in a chaotic environment. By clearing away the clutter and distractions in our homes, we make room and time for what is truly important.

It's nearly impossible to have an effective quiet time with the television blaring. It's difficult to build meaningful family memories in a room piled with dirty laundry. It's challenging to be truly hospitable to others when your guests can't walk across your floor without tripping over toys. And it's hard to teach children the important life skills of discipline and responsibility when you never require them to clean up their messes. Not to mention that for most mothers, a disorderly home creates tension and stress, which can negatively impact the entire family atmosphere.

Any environment can become a sanctuary that reflects God's nature of order, beauty, and peace—even a prison cell. I was greatly inspired by the example of Betsie ten Boom. She and her sister, Corrie, were thrown into a Nazi prison for hiding Jews in their home during the Holocaust. Betsie had always had a gift for making things beautiful, for making a house into a haven. But could a prison cell be made into a haven? Corrie described walking past Betsie's cell and getting a glimpse of the sanctuary that she had created there.

"Unbelievably, against all logic, the cell was charming," Corrie wrote. "The straw pallets were rolled instead of piled in a heap, standing like little pillars among the walls, each with a lady's hat atop it. A headscarf had somehow been hung along the wall. The contents of several food packages were arranged on a small shelf. . . . Even the coats hanging on their hooks were part of the welcome of that room, each sleeve draped over the shoulder of the coat next to it like a row of dancing children."[5]

Whenever I feel that I'm lacking in money or proper tools for organizing or decorating my home, I remind myself that if Betsie ten Boom could make a prison cell into a sanctuary, I have no excuses for not building my home into one—even if I don't have a wad of money to spend on supplies and décor.

As you seek to make your home into a sanctuary for your family, remember that you don't need a huge house or a lot of resources. You just need to work creatively with what you *do* have, with the simple goal of reflecting the joy and peace of Christ, rather than attempting to achieve the "fairy-tale perfection" of Pinterest or *Martha Stewart Living*.

Remember, the attitude in your home is far more important than the material things in your home. Four simple walls and a ceiling can easily be turned into a beautiful haven of peace with a little focus and effort. Ask God to give you His creative ideas for how you can transform your home into a sanctuary for your family. If you create order and peace in your home as an act of love and obedience to Him, He will grant you everything you need to succeed!

## MAKING IT PRACTICAL

I don't pretend to be an expert when it comes to home organizing or decorating. Many great books, websites, and blogs offer inspiring and practical tips in these areas, and I often turn to those resources for ideas (though I limit my exposure to these mediums, so that I don't become obsessed with homemaking perfectionism!). But to pass on a bit of what has helped me, I would like to share a few simple ways I have applied the principle of sanctuary in my own home:

## 1. MAKE YOUR KIDS' BEDROOMS PLACES OF BEAUTY AND ORDER

It can be challenging to make a small child's bedroom a place of beauty and order. Most affordable children's furniture is characterized by cheap plastic, obnoxiously bright colors, and tacky images of Dora the Explorer or SpongeBob. On top of that, kids are always toting around random items and leaving them on the bedroom floor. It's not uncommon for me to find a squishy toy elephant, an old paintbrush, and the lid to a Tupperware container lying next to my six-year-old's bed, or a bunch of ripped-out pages from an *Oriental Trading* catalog on the floor of my eight-year-old's room. I understand why many moms throw up their hands and resign themselves to the notion that kids' bedrooms are destined to be haphazard and cluttered.

Here's how I've tackled this challenge:

I wanted to turn my daughters' room into a soothing, peaceful, feminine retreat; a place where they could learn to be little ladies. I shopped around to find the right colors for the bedding and décor—soft and springtime fresh, with a few splashes of bold pink. I wanted to capture both girls' unique personalities: Avy's energetic spunkiness and Harper's delicate grace. I hung their names in wooden letters over each girl's bed, making that corner of the room especially "hers." (There is just something about a child seeing his or her name lovingly displayed that makes that child feel extra special!) I found some sweet, inexpensive paper butterflies at a craft store to pin on the walls. With my mom's help, I found a secondhand child's table and painted it white with pink embellishments, and a single silk rose adorns the tabletop. This is where the girls like to sit and read books or pretend to have tea. I placed labeled bins inside the girls' closet for them to store their toys. Each morning (unless we are rushing) I work with Avy and Harper to help them make their beds, put away their dirty clothes, and find a hiding place for all the little odds and ends they manage to collect. One of my best solutions for corralling clutter was putting a small decorative basket near each of their beds, as a catchall for odds and ends, such as ribbons, scraps of paper, barrettes, pencils, crayons, plastic animals, and all the other small, random items that always seem to appear out of nowhere around the bedroom.

I did something similar in the boys' rooms. I found a world-traveler-style trunk to place at the foot of each of their beds, where our little explorers can stash extra toys, stuffed animals, and knickknacks that they have collected. In the past, I've decorated their rooms with themes of trucks, cars, or animals, but as they grew older, I wanted to do something more meaningful. Our vision is that our boys will become God's little heroes, marked by bravery and tenacity. I wanted to remind them of these virtues each time they entered their special "boy rooms." We adorned their walls with prints that portray the daring exploits of the knights of the Round Table and the bravery of William Wallace. We hung wooden letters on the walls that spell words like *Hero, Courage,* and *Brave.* A few swords and shields embellish the walls as well. And we used rich chocolate-browns and reds for the bedding and décor to make the rooms as "manly" as possible. I wanted the design of their rooms to be a constant reminder of the mighty rescuers God is shaping them into.

✱ ✱ ✱

This doesn't mean that my children's rooms never look like a tornado hit them or that we never have times when the beds don't get made for a few days. However, I've found that when our kids' rooms are clean, beautiful, and purposefully decorated, it helps make bedtime, naptime, and playtime enjoyable for parents and children alike. This motivates me to train my kids to keep their rooms clean and clutter free.

## 2. SET UP AN INSPIRING AND ORDERLY CLASSROOM

One of my biggest fears about homeschooling was that I would not enjoy it and that it would become a tedious chore for both the kids and me. I envisioned them doing school in their pajamas around a messy kitchen table with schoolbooks that were caked with jelly smudges and bits of scrambled egg. I knew that if I dreaded teaching my kids each day, that attitude would filter down to them. I wanted my children to look forward to learning, so they would give their best to their studies and reach their potential. I wanted to bring fun, excitement, and dignity to their learning experience, but at first I wasn't sure how to accomplish this.

After talking for a while, Eric and I decided the first step was to set up a beautiful and orderly learning environment. The most practical area for a schoolroom was in the basement because it meant we could keep art supplies, books, and kid-clutter out of the main flow of the house. But we wanted our kids' learning environment to be as fresh, inviting, and well lit as possible, so that they would love being in school. We didn't feel we could achieve those goals if we used the basement as our classroom. So, we had to get creative in finding the right space. We decided to turn our attached garage into a large playroom/classroom. It is right off the kitchen, has ample room for everyone to spread out, and boasts plenty of windows to let in the refreshing sunlight throughout the day.

We didn't have a large budget (due to all the construction costs from turning our garage into a finished space!) so we scoured secondhand stores and tried to be creative. My mom and I found a huge bulletin board for five dollars that we could use to hide some ugly electrical boxes on the wall. We covered it with cute fabric, and it became an art display area for the kids' masterpieces. To cut down on craft-supply clutter, we filled two white bookshelves with cute bins and baskets and attached wooden chalkboard labels to each one to announce its contents. I ordered four child-size school desks so each of our kids would have a learning space of his or her own. I found a large desk at a thrift store, painted it white, and put new hardware on it to make it into a "teacher's desk" where

I could do my lesson planning. I placed an inexpensive table in the center of the room for craft projects and filled mason jars with crayons, pencils, and art supplies. As the room came together, I gained newfound vision and eagerness to teach my kids every day.

If you are homeschooling your kids, take an inventory of your home and try to find a place that can be transformed into an organized, beautiful classroom. Having a designated classroom space can bring beauty, purpose, focus, and dignity to the process of teaching your children at home. It might be a little-used dining room or formal living room, a nook off the kitchen, a corner of the family room, or even an area of the basement that can be freshened up with good lighting and décor. With a little focus and creativity, you can set up a classroom that will bring beauty, purpose, focus, and dignity to the homeschooling experience.

Last year our kids started attending a part-time tutoring program through our church, so I'm no longer teaching them at home all day, every day. However, even on the days that we are not officially homeschooling, we still use our classroom for reading, art, and special projects. Whether you are homeschooling full-time or not, having a designated learning space at home greatly benefits kids as they discover, play, and create.

3. TURN THE MASTER BEDROOM INTO A MARRIAGE SANCTUARY

When you are a busy mom of young children, it's easy to make the little ones your highest priority and let your relationship with your husband take a backseat when it comes to your focus and attention. But kids quickly start feeling insecure when they sense a lack of unity and affection between their mom and dad. For a family to thrive, a husband and wife's relationship must be healthy and strong.

One of the best ways to make your marriage a priority during the child-raising years is to turn your bedroom into a sacred retreat, where you and your husband can go to be alone, talk, pray, and cultivate your relationship together. Whenever the kids have felt the freedom to adorn our master bedroom with their toys, books, artwork, and other treasures, or to hang out there anytime they want, Eric and I have lost focus, priority, and privacy in our relationship. So it has become my goal to keep the bedroom set apart for our marriage and to quarantine the kids' belongings and activities to other areas of the house.

Even if you are a single mom, you will benefit from making your bedroom a private retreat where you can take time to be alone, refresh, and refocus. Our bedroom is the one quiet place in our house where I can journal, pray, or read without constant interruption. Without that quiet haven, it would be far more challenging to handle the noise and intensity of life with four little kids.

This doesn't mean we never allow the kids into our room. Sometimes we let them pile up on our king-size bed to read them stories or to watch an edifying movie together as a family. We nearly always let them sleep on the couch in our room when they are sick or if they wake up in the night with a bad dream. But for the most part, we keep our bedroom purposed for a marriage retreat, instead of letting it be the kids' adventure land or dumping ground.

Our bedroom has taken on many different looks over the years, but here are some of the basic principles I follow when it comes to setting up the master bedroom as a marriage sanctuary:

*1. Consider his tastes.* When you are single, your bedroom can be as girly as you prefer, but once you are married, it's important to make the bedroom a place that captures both feminine *and* masculine preferences. Choose colors and décor that both you and your spouse like, something neutral instead of frilly and feminine. Sure, you can have a few flowers and feminine touches around the master bedroom, but be careful not to make it look like a rose garden or trendy "diva's hangout." Even if your husband doesn't have an opinion about colors and decorating, you can still try to incorporate his likes, tastes, and unique personality as you are choosing the décor. Make the bedroom feel like his retreat just as much as it is yours.

*2. Keep it clean.* Make your bed every day, as soon as you wake up. Let this become just as much a habit as brushing your teeth. An unmade bed makes the whole room feel sloppy and unromantic. Keep attractive baskets in strategic locations so that you can easily stash random items that might have migrated in from other areas of the house. Don't let clutter remain on the dressers or nightstands. If you don't have time to put everything in its proper place each day, keep a catchall basket that you clean out once a week so that mail, magazines, and mismatched socks don't pile up.

*3. Remove distractions.* Don't allow television, computers, video games, work projects, or other distractions into your bedroom. We don't have a television in our house at all (except for the monitor we use to watch edifying movies with our kids every once in a while), and the atmosphere in our home is much healthier and more peaceful as a result. Instead of using media or the Internet to help you and your spouse "unwind" after a long day, turn to spiritually edifying and relationship-building activities such as praying, talking, or reading a great book together.

Eric and I keep a supply of spiritually enriching books and Christian biographies in our room, which makes it that much easier to read together in the evenings. Reading these kinds of books, as well as praying and talking together about what God is doing in our lives, keeps our marriage relationship strong, thriving, and built upon the right foundation. Do your best to keep distractions out of the bedroom so that you and your husband can focus on God and each other whenever you spend time in your private retreat. Otherwise, the bedroom will become just another room in the house.

\* \* \*

As the keepers of our homes, we have a choice to make about the atmosphere we create for our families. We can either build a lifestyle that reflects heaven's beauty and order or one that showcases this world's selfish, chaotic frenzy. Family relationships cannot be cultivated in the midst of rushed, harried schedules, cluttered houses, and microwave dinners eaten hastily while watching reality television. Romance doesn't thrive with husbands sacked out in the Barcalounger in front of the nightly news and wives chasing screaming kids around the house.

To build your home into a sanctuary (and maintain it) requires discipline. As a godly mother who "watches over the ways of her house," you must become a vigilant guardian, ready to purge out any influences and distractions that creep into your home and undermine your family. Creating a haven of peace in your home requires proactive, purposeful focus and energy; it's not something that will happen by itself. Even if you don't feel gifted in this area, ask God to show you simple ways that you can do all things "decently and in order" in your home. If you build your life, focus, and motherhood around Christ, He will give you the grace to build a home environment that exudes beauty and reflects the order, peace, simplicity, and serenity of heaven.

## LET'S TALK ABOUT IT

*Group Study and Discussion*

1. **Read Genesis 1 and 1 Corinthians 14:40.** How do these verses demonstrate that God is a God who values order and beauty? How should this principle translate into how we manage our homes?

2. **Read Proverbs 14:1.** What does it mean to create a Christ-centered sanctuary instead of a self-centered "show home"? Have you ever been in a home that was truly a sanctuary of peace? What did you observe?

3. **Read 2 Corinthians 6:15-18.** What are some of the greatest threats to a Christ-centered sanctuary? How can we protect our homes from these threats?

## TAKE IT DEEPER

*Personal Study and Reflection*

**Read:** Titus 2:5
**Reflect:** Is my home a Christ-centered sanctuary? Are there ways in which I can bring more order and peace into my home? How would this impact my family?

**Read:** Hebrews 13:4
**Reflect:** Are there any areas in my home life where I'm putting my children above my marriage? What steps might God be asking me to take in order to change these patterns?

**Read:** Proverbs 16:18
**Reflect:** Am I seeking to honor Christ and serve my family in keeping an orderly home, or do I desire to impress others with my decorating and homemaking skills? Am I harboring any pride in this area of my life that God must gently expose and remove?

# CHAPTER FIVE

# ESTABLISHING A HEALTHY ROUTINE

*Guarding What's Truly Important*

*To everything there is a season, a time for every purpose under heaven.*

ECCLESIASTES 3:1

KATHERINE G. HOWARD, the mother of Elisabeth Elliot, once wrote this about the importance of order and structure in family life:

> There is a great deal of talk these days about having things "unstructured." Just how can a Christian make this jibe with such Scriptures as, "Let all things be done decently and in order" [1 Cor. 14:40], or with a careful study of God's creation? What would happen to the galaxies if they were unstructured? Certainly there should be order in the home.[6]

Order and structure are gifts from God that help us guard what is truly important in our lives. However, I must admit that creating a consistent routine for my family has proven to be one of the greatest challenges of my motherhood.

It's easy to feel stifled by the mere idea of being bound to a specific daily routine. Many mothers don't like the discipline and would much prefer to "go with the flow" each day rather than submit to a schedule. We often think a routine will limit our freedom and remove the fun from our lives.

But I have found the opposite to be true. While I believe that there should be a bit of spontaneity in family life, and that there will always be a level of unpredictability with kids, I also know that establishing a healthy routine is crucial in order for both children and mothers to thrive. Whenever I set a schedule for my kids and manage to stick with it, I actually find *more* freedom to focus on what's really important in life, such as cultivating intimacy with Christ, spending meaningful time with my family, and practicing hospitality. Having a routine helps guard these priorities. It also provides my children the security and structure they crave.

If I don't follow a daily routine, an entire week can go by before I realize I've had no time for prayer, quiet times, or meaningful time with my family. I've been too busy doing a bunch of "this and that" and dealing with extra discipline issues that arise because my kids feel unstable and off balance. Children thrive on routine, and so do mothers, no matter what personality God has given you!

When we appoint a specific, regular time each day for

the tasks and priorities God has given us, we won't get over-whelmed trying to figure out how to fit everything in or waste time with conflicts that arise when kids have too much free time on their hands. (Bored children = whining, pester-ing, mischief-seeking children!)

Of course, our family sometimes does things sponta-neously, and there are times when ministry or unexpected events demand that we temporarily set aside our routine. But whenever possible, I try to keep life predictable for my children. It greatly benefits the atmosphere and attitudes in our home when I succeed at this, and I have more stamina and energy when our family routine is in a healthy groove.

In her book *The Shaping of a Christian Family*, Elisabeth Elliot describes a cartoon scene from a Christian magazine where the mother is disheveled and harried, the children are wildly out of control, the cat and dog are tearing each other's ears off, and the father is watching helplessly. She contrasts this comical but all-too-common scenario with her own growing-up experience, in which her parents—especially her mother—put a strong emphasis on structure, routine, and stability:

> The regularity of our schedule was one of the things
> we depended on, and though we did not know it at
> the time, it gave us a great security. Mother made it
> a rule to get meals on the table when we expected
> them to be there. Our little world could be counted
> on to stay the way it was; safe, structured, and pretty

much the same every day. Whenever we burst in the door [after school], there was Mother, and there was the hot soup. It was nice to smell the soup, and it was nice that Mother was always there for us. Always.[7]

The decisions we make now can impact our children for the rest of their lives. If we fail to create an atmosphere of discipline, structure, and order for our children, we make it much more difficult for them to embrace these skills later in life. Having a routine helps kids learn important values such as punctuality, dependability, and healthy time management. It helps them feel secure in knowing what comes next in their day.

Of course, it's not a good idea to run our homes like a military academy. It's healthy to provide a measure of free time every day so that our children can have some spontaneity and serendipity in their lives. But if things are always unstructured, unscheduled, and "go with the flow," then we will rob our children of many crucial skills they need in order to succeed in life.

Too many moms try to maintain the same personal freedoms they had in their single years, expecting their kids to somehow fit into their unstructured and spur-of-the-moment lifestyle. They get irritated when their kids can't adapt to their spontaneous whims or when discipline issues arise at inconvenient moments and hamper their personal agenda. But for the sake of our children's hearts, minds, and futures, we must sacrifice certain freedoms when we become mothers. If you constantly drag your small children around with you as you window-shop, socialize, attend events, and meet friends for coffee, you are setting both yourself and your children up for frustration.

Children are the happiest when life is predictable.

In the Ludy home, we have tried to keep our nighttime routine more or less the same for the past couple of years. At a specific time of night, all the kids get into their pj's and have a small bedtime snack around the kitchen table. Then, a tooth-brushing party in the bathroom. Next, each child gets tucked in and prayed for. Mommy nearly always sings a song for each of the girls. ("The Cheetah Went over the Mountain" and "The Little Brown Church" are popular requests.) And then I tell a made-up story to each of the boys. (Usually, at the request of my eight-year-old, a zany tale involving a raccoon, a beaver, and a whale. The more nonsensical, the better.)

Eric has a special talk with each of the kids as they are drifting off to sleep, speaking words of truth and affirmation to them and praying for their dreams. Each of the kids has a specific way that he or she likes to be tucked in. Harper always wants two Kleenexes under her pillow (never one or three!) and her beloved Lambie by her side. Avy always wants her special pink blanket and fluffy purple pillow. Kipling wants his "daddy lion" and "baby bear" next to him. And Hudson likes his favorite stuffed dog, Rusty, and cozy "blue blankie," his loyal companions since babyhood. All of them want a bottle of water by their beds and their bedroom doors cracked open just the right way.

As a general rule, Eric and I say no to speaking and ministry commitments that require both of us to be away from the children at night. We try to make sure at least one of us is home to carry out the nighttime ritual that our children are used to, rather than having a babysitter put them to bed. (On the few occasions that we must both be away from the kids for a night, they usually go on a "vacation" across town to their grandparents' house, which is kind of like Disneyland for them!)

It can be an inconvenience to build our schedule around our kids' bedtime every night, and it limits the number of social events, ministry opportunities, and other activities we can be involved in. But the peace, order, and serenity that this nighttime routine provides for our kids makes the sacrifice well worth it.

Whenever possible, we have regular bedtimes, rest times, wake-up times, and mealtimes. My kids know when it is "art time," "school time," "playtime," and "book time." For a while, we even had a twenty-minute period of time right after breakfast that my eight-year-old organized and called "roundup time"—when he would round up all the kids to show them an educational video in the classroom while I took some time to get organized for my teaching with the kids.

I try to avoid having too many moments in the day when my kids wander around the house, looking for ways to entertain themselves. Proverbs 29:15 says, "A child left to himself brings shame to his mother." I have witnessed this truth first-hand many times! When I let my kids fend for themselves, they nearly always find something destructive to do, such as pouring an entire bucket of plastic beads into the bathtub, decorating the sink with nail polish, or pestering the dog.

To avoid these scenarios, I have found it works best to give my kids a specific room in the house to play in (or a specific area of the yard, such as the sandbox) and a defined group of toys to play with. (For example, "The bucket of army guys and bin of plastic animals are okay to play with, but let's save the Legos, play food, tea set, pretend instruments, dress-up clothes, and wooden blocks for next time.") When I don't give my kids specific boundaries, playtime quickly gets out of control and morphs into a toy explosion all around the house. And when my kids are given too many options and choices, it leads to scattered attention spans. The older and more mature my children become, the more freedom and flexibility I am able to give them. But first they must prove faithful in "a very little thing" so they can be entrusted with more (Lk. 16:10, NASB).

My oldest son enjoys making home videos and creating funny digital stories on the computer. But rather than letting him wander into the office and work on the computer whenever the mood strikes, I try to give him a designated "computer time" each day. Usually his "computer time" coincides with the other children's rest time, which allows me to have some time each afternoon when the house is quiet and I can get things done or close my eyes for a few minutes.

In the late afternoons, we try to do a physical activity such as tennis, bike riding, or playtime at the park. In the evenings, we eat dinner together around the same time, take care of household chores, and spend time together. For the most part, we keep our weeknights free of social events and other activities so we can protect our sacred family time.

We don't follow an extremely rigid schedule in any of these areas, but we strive to keep things relatively predictable. Our routine provides the stability and order that our family needs to not just survive but to thrive.

To be honest, I do not always feel like a roaring success in preserving our family's routine. It often seems that no sooner do I establish a consistent rhythm to our daily life than something unexpected happens to throw everything off. And the neatly organized flowchart I have posted on the refrigerator serves as a shameful reminder that I am not sticking to the routine the way I had intended.

When this happens, I've learned not to wallow in guilt or frustration but to simply modify the routine the best I can to fit the unique season we are walking through and to keep things as consistent as possible, even if it's not picture-perfect. Then, when things settle down again, I get back to the routine as quickly as possible.

## MAKING IT PRACTICAL

There are many practical ways to create a healthy routine for your family. In fact, there are entire books written on the subject, many of which are excellent resources and go into far more detail than I can cover in this chapter. (See the recommended resources on page 157 for some of my favorites.) However, I'd like to share some of the most helpful principles God has taught me in the area of guarding what's truly important in family life.

## 1. PRACTICE PERSONAL DISCIPLINE

I have found that personal discipline is key to my ability to create a healthy routine for my kids. If my own life is haphazard and chaotic, my kids' routine quickly falls by the wayside.

As a busy mother with many demands on my time, attention, emotions, and energy, there is a constant bait to become lax in my sleep habits, computer time, and social life. It's easy to linger in bed just a little too long in the morning and then have to scramble around trying to catch up for the rest of the day. It's tempting to spend just a little too much time browsing the Internet or attending to my e-mails, squandering time that should have been spent on more important things, such as nurturing my children. When a friend calls unexpectedly, it's easy to stay on the phone longer than necessary, robbing time that should have been given to household tasks or child training.

And the most dangerous of all the temptations is letting my spiritual life fall by the wayside. Instead of rising early to seek God or spending time in prayer at night after my children are asleep, I can easily be tempted to fill those hours with extra sleep or other indulgences. Self-Pity whispers,

*You've been working so hard; you deserve a little "me time" right now. You can always pray later.* While there is nothing wrong with sleep, fun activities, or alone time, these things should never take priority over my relationship with Christ or my prayer life.

When prayer is missing from our lives, when sleep and laziness control us, we spend endless time and energy trying to make our lives work. But as it says in Psalm 1, when we meditate upon our Lord day and night, we become like a tree that brings forth much fruit, and everything that we do prospers. Our time is multiplied. Our effectiveness is multiplied. Our energy is multiplied. Life becomes fruitful instead of frustrating. On two different occasions, the disciples fished all night long and caught nothing. But when Jesus came and stood in their midst, they merely had to let down their net once and they caught such an abundance that they didn't have room in their boat to contain it all (see Lk. 5:4-6; Jn. 21:3-6).

Many moms with small children complain that they do not have time to spend in prayer and seeking God. I certainly won't pretend that having young children makes spiritual discipline easy! However, there is almost always a way to make time with God a priority if we really want to. Often, it just means adding a little (or a lot!) more discipline to our lives. For instance, how many hours each day do you spend on the computer, on Facebook, or on the phone? How much time do you spend in front of television or movies each night to decompress from your busy day? Would you be willing to reduce or even eliminate these activities in order to spend time in God's presence?

Take a prayerful and honest look at your daily life. Are there areas in which you need greater personal discipline? Are there activities that need to be eliminated or cut back in order to put more priority on what's important? Is laziness hindering your relationship with God? Is your social life undermining your ability to train and nurture your children? Are you spending more time tweeting, blogging, or posting photos on Instagram than you are actually being a mother to your kids? If you identify areas that need to change, ask God to grant you the grace and practical wisdom to take the steps that are necessary. He will be faithful to lead you and guide you.

Discipline is not something that can be gained in one night. It requires training, dedication, and consistency in order to become habitual in your daily life. For example, if you are working toward an earlier wake-up time, start with small steps and gradually work up to bigger goals. If you are used to waking up at 9 a.m. and you try to suddenly switch to a 5 a.m. wake-up time, chances are you will wane in your commitment after a day or two. Instead, try setting your alarm for twenty minutes earlier for the first couple of days. Then, set it for another twenty minutes earlier and work on that new discipline for a few days. Continue this pattern until you have reached the wake-up time that you feel God is asking of you. Let your body get used to change over a period of a few weeks, rather than biting off more than you can chew in one day.

In addition to training and consistency, adding discipline to your life also requires an infusion of the enabling grace of God. And it takes faith to believe that change is possible —"according to the power that works in us" (Eph. 3:20). The apostle Paul said, "I discipline my body and bring it into subjection, lest, when I have preached to others, I myself should become disqualified" (1 Cor. 9:27). Even Paul had to build godly discipline into his life in order to keep his ministry sharp and Christ focused.

When we run the race with patience, the rewards are off-the-charts amazing. A life built around God's priorities is the most fulfilling life we could ever imagine.

## 2. BE PROACTIVE IN CHILD TRAINING

We cannot expect babysitters, schoolteachers, or day-care workers to be the primary means of character training for our kids. God has given that sacred responsibility to parents. I remember once hearing a child-training expert say, "Don't expect your child to demonstrate proper behavior in public if he's not being trained in that behavior at home." In other words, it is unfair for us to get frustrated with our kids when they don't behave properly at church or in the grocery store when we have not been consistently working with them in those areas at home.

When our oldest son was about six, he would look at the ground and remain unresponsive whenever an adult tried to engage him in conversation. I was embarrassed and frustrated by his lack of social skills, until one day it dawned on me that

I'd never really taught him the basics of proper interpersonal communication. So I set up some "training sessions" for Hudson at home, in which my husband and I would practice asking him questions and teaching him how to smile, look the other person in the eye, and give a friendly response. It took a few times of doing this before the lessons really sank in, but eventually Hudson became much more interactive whenever adults spoke to him in public.

I've learned firsthand that social gatherings are the wrong time to train my children in proper manners and respectful behavior. Rather, social gatherings are opportunities to practice and reinforce the manners and behavior I have been instilling into my children at home.

Be sure to build a daily routine that allows you to take a proactive role in character and behavior training for your children. A child can't learn the skill of sitting still when life is moving so fast that the family rarely sits at the table and eats a meal together. Children won't develop the habits of making their beds or keeping their rooms clean when everyone oversleeps each morning and then makes a mad scramble to get out the door on time. Kids can't develop healthy sleep patterns if we let them stay up until all hours and then collapse on the couch in exhaustion every night. That's why it's important to keep your long-term child-training goals in mind when you are planning your day-to-day schedule.

Eric and I learned early on in our parenting that unless we took an assertive role in training, directing, and disciplining our children, their self-centered agendas would rule the atmosphere of our home. When our first child was born, we decided, "Hudson must learn how to become *part* of our family, not the center of it." I'll admit that this approach is much harder work for the parent, especially at first. It's much easier in the moment to just give in to a whining, screaming, demanding child than take the time to train him or her to yield to your will. After all, if you can make a child stop crying by giving him or her a cookie, why would you resort instead to a twenty-five-minute training session involving conflict and tears?

But children learn to submit to their parent's authority, and ultimately to God's authority, through faithful, proactive, godly training. If we take the easy road and give in to our children's demands without taking time to teach them how to obey, submit, and respect authority, we are failing in our responsibility as parents.

It's important to note that the purpose of godly child-training is not so that we can impress the world with our well-behaved children. Rather, God asks us to train our children in His ways so that they will be prepared to yield their hearts and lives fully to Him (see Dt. 11:19-21; Prov. 22:6; 23:13-14).

Whatever stage of growth and development your children are in, ask God to show you which areas of godly character training are most important for you to focus on. For example, does your baby need to learn healthy eating and sleeping patterns so that his inconsistency isn't throwing off

*Great idea*

the entire household? Does your toddler need to learn how to cheerfully obey your requests instead of throwing a fit when she doesn't get her way? Does your preschooler need to learn how to wait respectfully instead of interrupting you when you are talking with someone? (That one is a big focus in the Ludy home right now!) Does your older child need to learn diligence in his schoolwork?

I've found that it's helpful to write down specific child-training objectives and to post them in a place where I can see them each day, such as the fridge. Then, I am continually reminded to look for creative, healthy ways to teach those behaviors to my kids and to build my daily routine around my child-training goals. (For some of my favorite child-training resources, please see page 157.)

As your children grow and develop, you will need to adapt your routine according to their changing needs. But remember that making the effort to build a schedule that allows you to be actively involved in your child's spiritual growth and character training will lay the foundation for success in every area of his or her life.

Loving our kids well means more than just enjoying their cuteness and taking care of their basic needs. It means sacrificially, diligently, consistently training them in the ways of God. As it says in Proverbs 31:26, a godly mother has "wisdom" and "the law of kindness" on her tongue.

Making time for what's truly important in family life is

not always easy. But when you look back in twenty, thirty, or forty years, you will be able to confidently say that it was worth every bit of sacrifice!

## LET'S TALK ABOUT IT

*Group Study and Discussion*

1. **Read Ecclesiastes 3:1; 3:11; and Galatians 4:4.** Since God has an appointed time for everything, how should this principle impact our homes and family lives?

2. **Read Proverbs 16:9.** Why do we often resist the idea of structure and routine? What is the difference between a legalistic schedule and a healthy routine? How can a healthy routine benefit our families?

3. **Read 1 Timothy 5:13.** What are some of the biggest threats to keeping our families in a healthy daily rhythm? How can we protect our families from these threats?

## TAKE IT DEEPER

*Personal Study and Reflection*

**Read:** Proverbs 16:3

**Reflect:** Am I building my daily plans around God's agenda or my own? Are there areas of my daily life that need to adjust around God's priorities? If so, which areas?

**Read:** Philippians 2:4
**Reflect:** Do I expect my children to adapt around my own selfish whims and spontaneous desires? Are there personal sacrifices I need to make in order to provide more stability to my children's daily routine?

**Read:** Proverbs 22:6
**Reflect:** Am I being proactive in training my children in God's ways? Are there any changes I need to make to my daily routine in order to train them diligently, as God asks me to?

# CHAPTER SIX

# TENDING TO THEIR SOULS

*Sharing the Gospel with Your Children*

*Assuredly, I say to you, unless you are converted and become as little children, you will by no means enter the kingdom of heaven.*

MATTHEW 18:3

I WILL NEVER forget the moment when Hudson gave his life to Jesus. He and Eric had been pulling weeds together in the backyard, and Eric began talking with him about spiritual things and about the condition of his soul. Our son, though only six, was responsive and attentive, which in hindsight can only be attributed to the grace of God, since Hudson had an extremely short attention span at that time in his life. Eric lovingly and thoroughly explained the gospel to Hudson. About two hours later, Hudson understood his complete and utter need for a Savior, and he asked Jesus Christ to wash him clean and take over his life.

There is no greater joy for a Christian parent than seeing your children come into the kingdom of God. Children have a trusting faith and readiness to understand and receive the gospel unlike at any other time in their lives. It's up to us as parents to sow the seeds of truth into this fertile ground, while we have the chance. It's easy to get sidetracked with tending to our kids' health, social development, education, and athletic interests. All these things are certainly valuable, but if we never tend to their souls, we will overlook the most important need in their lives.

Many Christian parents today focus on instilling godly character in their children but fail to introduce them to the person of Jesus Christ. I believe that character training is of great importance in a child's life, as I shared in the previous chapter. But if we never help them cultivate a personal, intimate, daily relationship with Christ, then all our character training will be meaningless in the long run. All the character training, Bible knowledge, and church activities in the world can never replace a genuine, personal relationship with Jesus Christ.

Studies show that a disturbingly large number of young people who have grown up in Christian homes have left the faith by the time they graduate from college.[8] Many of these young people had godly parents who spent years training them in godly behaviors. They attended Sunday school and church. They went to youth group and had Christian friends. And yet, they never made a covenant exchange with the King of all kings; they never gave their lives to Jesus and entered into a personal, life-transforming relationship with Him.

We have the opportunity and privilege of leading our children into a relationship with Christ and helping them make that relationship the foundation of every godly behavior in their lives. In their early years, our children must be taught to comply with correct behavior simply to respect the requirements and expectations of their parents and other authorities. But our ultimate goal should be for our children to turn their lives wholeheartedly over to Jesus Christ and to embrace godly behavior out of a heartfelt desire to love, honor, and please their King.

A lot of Christian parents I've known think that others are more qualified than they are to share the truth of Jesus Christ with their kids. It's tempting to believe that if our kids attend Sunday school and Bible clubs, they'll be introduced to the gospel, which can then be reinforced at home. But this is backward reasoning. God has entrusted *us* with the privilege of leading our little ones to Christ (see Eph. 6:4). Following Jesus is the most crucial decision our children will ever make—the decision that will determine their eternal fate. Who better to facilitate this all-important decision than us as parents, the ones who have been anointed and appointed by God for this sacred task?

This doesn't mean that Sunday school and Bible clubs are to be avoided. Outside Christian influences can be a wonderful tool to help shape your children's spiritual growth and development. But parents should take the lead in giving their kids a strong foundation in the gospel, and outside Christian influences should merely be tools to reinforce the truth they are receiving at home.

Remember, no matter how unqualified you may feel, God has specifically called *you* to lead your children to Him. If you ask Him to equip you and lead you, He will provide all of the wisdom, creativity, and diligence you need to point your children's hearts to Christ. I love the following quote by R. A. Torrey:

> Oh, mothers and fathers, it is your privilege to have every one of your children saved. But it costs something to have them saved. It costs your spending much time alone with God, to be much in prayer, and it costs also your making those sacrifices and straightening out those things in your life that are wrong; it costs the fulfilling the conditions of prevailing prayer. And if any of you have unsaved children, when you go home today get alone with God and ask God to show you what it is in your own life that is responsible for the present condition of your children.[9]

Let us not fail to make the eternal salvation of our children the highest priority of our parenting and to make whatever personal sacrifices necessary in order to lead them to Christ.

## MAKING IT PRACTICAL

Here are some principles that my husband and I found helpful when sharing the gospel with our kids.

### 1. DON'T SUGARCOAT TRUTH

We first began speaking to our children about the gospel when they were quite young, between the ages of four and six. When talking with this age group, it's tempting to focus only on the happy aspects of the gospel and downplay the notions of sin, death, and hell. After all, we don't want to upset our kids with matters that their little minds are not ready for! But if children never recognize the seriousness of sin and the horrible destiny that awaits those who do not know Jesus Christ, their hearts will not be prepared to understand the "good news" of the gospel. So it's important not to sugarcoat the truth. Kids need to be disturbed over their sin. They need to recognize their helplessness to be clean and justified before God. And they need to understand the misery of hell. Before they can grasp the good news, they must fully comprehend the bad news.

Last summer, we had a Sunday morning "church service" in our living room, with only our family present. My husband and I spent about two hours walking through the gospel with our three youngest children.

We started out with the story of Adam and Eve and the saddest day in history when sin entered the world. We talked about the perfect righteousness and holiness of God and how no one can come into His presence unless they are perfect too. We talked about sin and what sin does in our lives. We talked about the "place of pain," where sinners will spend eternity separated from God. Along the way, the children interrupted to ask questions or repeat things back to us, and we found ourselves clarifying and re-explaining things a few times. But overall, they seemed to grasp the seriousness of the "bad news."

They began to spontaneously confess different sins they had committed—disobedience, lying, and even stealing (our youngest son admitted to taking a Matchbox car from the church toy bin when he was three). As they recognized how sinful they were, they began to understand that they could never get to heaven on their own. They were quiet as this fact became clear.

Then we introduced them to the wonderful, incredible, jubilant reality of the gospel. How Jesus Christ, "who knew no sin," became a sacrifice for us to make a way to the Father (2 Cor. 5:21). How He took our place on the cross and bore the punishment that should have been ours. What glorious news! The kids were excited to recognize how much Jesus loved them and how much He had sacrificed for them.

Then we explained what it means to be "in Christ." We told them what it means to be washed clean by His blood, to turn our lives over to His rulership, and to be clothed in His righteousness. They were happy and excited as they realized what an amazing gift Jesus was offering to each of them.

One by one, they took turns praying, confessing their sin, and expressing their desire for Jesus Christ to forgive them, wash them clean, and take over their lives. At the end of the prayer, something was different. They felt a newfound life and freedom and a security in knowing that they now belonged to Jesus. Ever since that day, they boldly declare that they are "in Christ" and that they will be with Him in heaven someday.

Sharing the gospel with children is a lot more than getting them to say a "sinner's prayer." It took a little over two hours for us to walk through the gospel with our kids. This is because we took the time to walk through the seriousness of sin and the reality of hell, the redemptive gift of salvation, and what it means to truly be "in Christ." At very young ages, children may not be able to grasp all the depths of the saving power of Christ. But they are capable of comprehending more than we give them credit for. It is vital that we don't shortchange them on the truths that will help them really understand the sacred covenant exchange they are making when they give their lives to Jesus.

If you need help in grasping the reality of the gospel, I encourage you to listen to the messages "In Christ," and "The Carpetbag Gospel" available for download at www.ellerslie.com/sermons/archive. Meditating on the powerful work of the Cross is a wonderful way to prepare your heart and mind to teach this vital truth to your children.

2. REMIND THEM OF THEIR POSITION IN CHRIST
As they are newly planted in Christ, our children need to learn the principle of reckoning themselves "dead indeed to

sin, but alive to God in Christ Jesus our Lord"—the concept of the "old man" and the "new man" (see Ro. 6:8-13). When Eric and I see a sinful behavior pattern surfacing in their lives, we will often ask our kids where "old Kipling" or "old Harper" is. We remind them that their "old man" is dead and buried, that they are now "new Kipling" or "new Harper" who is in Christ Jesus. In their new position "in Christ," they have the power to "reckon [themselves] dead indeed to sin, but alive to God in Christ Jesus our Lord" (Ro. 6:11).

This may sound like a complicated truth for preschoolers to grasp, but we have found that our kids truly do "get it." They are aware of the difference between their "old" and "new" man. The old man has no ability to overcome sin. But now that they have been made new, old behavior patterns no longer have to control them. Through Christ, they have been given the power to choose right behavior over sin. When we remind them of these truths often, we see an incredible difference in the way they live.

This doesn't mean we have perfect children. (Wouldn't that be nice?!) But they are beginning to understand that sin no longer needs to have power over them.

When my youngest son begins to whine and resist obeying, I appeal to his understanding of the gospel. "Remember that you are 'new Kipling,'" I will remind him. "You can ask Jesus for the grace to say no to sin right now. You are in Christ, Kipling. Disobedience no longer needs to control you. Jesus has given you the power to say no to sin and choose what is right."

Often, these words will motivate him to stop the downward spiral he's on and ask for the grace to behave like "new Kipling" who is in "Christ Jesus." Frequently there is a marked difference in his attitude after I've taken the time to remind him of these truths. It's a marvelous thing to watch God at work in his little soul.

When you are working with your kids' behavior issues, don't stop short and rely only on discipline and character-training principles. Incorporate the message of the gospel, and frequently remind them that they belong to Jesus Christ. As they grow and develop, the victory and power of the gospel will become an unshakable foundation in their lives.

### 3. HELP THEM CULTIVATE INTIMACY WITH CHRIST

Children won't learn the spiritual disciplines of prayer, Bible study, and seeking God unless we model it for them and provide opportunities for them to practice these things. Our older son has a quiet time each morning, in which he listens to the *Word of Promise* audio Bible through his headphones, while following along reading the same passage in his Bible. Seeing and hearing Scripture at the same time helps him grasp it at a much deeper level. At breakfast, we often spend a few minutes letting him share what he's learning from the Word of God.

With our younger kids, we are working on the basics of prayer. We model prayer for them and then invite them to pray. Sometimes they just go through the motions. But other times, there is a genuine and heartfelt "casting their burdens" on the One who cares for them (see 1 Pet. 5:7) and a precious demonstration of childlike faith.

We try to start each day with prayer and discussions about spiritual truths and end each day with worship and prayer. Whenever fears, behavioral issues, or conflicts arise, our goal is to point our kids back to their personal relationship with Jesus Christ and to teach them to immediately turn to Him for anything and everything they need. Are they afraid? *Let's pray and ask Jesus to give you His peace and remind you that He is always with you.* Are they angry? *Let's ask Jesus to change your heart right now so you can forgive your sister the way He forgave you.* Did they do something sinful and disobedient? *Let's think about how that makes Jesus feel. What should you do to make things right in your relationship with Him?*

About a year ago, our youngest son was having trouble falling asleep because he was scared of bad dreams and of being alone in his room. Leaving the hall light on with the door cracked open only provided a small amount of comfort. I reminded him that Jesus was always with him, watching over him, and that if he was scared, all he needed to do was ask Jesus to give him peace.

Kipling seemed comforted by this revelation, but he wanted some additional reinforcement. "Can you get me a picture of Jesus watching over me, so I can hang it up in my room?" he wanted to know. Since it was about 9 p.m. and Eric was out of town, it was impossible for me to go out shopping for a Jesus picture. I told Kipling to wait for a few minutes while I tried to find an image online that I could print out. After a little bit of searching, I found the perfect picture—a beautiful image of Jesus comforting a small boy, who just happened to look almost exactly like Kipling! I quickly printed it out and took it to his room.

As soon as he saw it, a huge smile creased his face, and he declared, "Yep, Jesus is watching over me all right!" Then he asked me to tape it on the window next to his bed. As soon as I did, he fell peacefully asleep.

Children are usually eager and ready to build a personal relationship with Christ. They respond to spiritual truths with a simple, uncomplicated faith. All we must do is take the opportunities in front of us each and every day and continually point their hearts to the One who loves them more than we ever could.

*     *     *

If sharing the gospel with your children and discipling them in the Christian life feels overwhelming, ask Jesus for specific guidance and grace. He will be faithful to show you what to say and when to say it. Remember, He cares about your children's souls even more than you do! And while you have been given the privilege of leading your children to Christ, it is He Himself who must accomplish that miracle within their souls. You are simply a vessel in His faithful hands.

## LET'S TALK ABOUT IT

*Group Study and Discussion*

1. **Read Matthew 18:3.** How are children uniquely ready to receive the gospel of Christ? How can we take advantage of the opportunity to reach their hearts with truth while they are young and receptive?

2. **Read Deuteronomy 6:6-7.** What are some of the most effective ways you've seen biblical truth shared with children? How can we apply the principles of Deuteronomy 6:6-7 in our homes?

3. **Read Proverbs 31:26 and Ephesians 6:4.** Why are parents uniquely equipped for sharing the gospel with their kids?

## TAKE IT DEEPER

*Personal Study and Reflection*

**Read:** Mark 16:15
**Reflect:** Am I fulfilling the Great Commission in my own home? Do I need to devote more time and energy to sharing the gospel with my children?

**Read:** Hebrews 3:13
**Reflect:** Am I diligently leading my children closer to Christ and helping them build a daily relationship with Him? What are some practical steps God might be asking me to take to become stronger in this area?

**Read:** Romans 6:11

**Reflect:** Am I applying this vital truth of the gospel in my own life? Have I "reckoned" myself "dead to sin," or do I believe that sin still has power to control me? Are there steps God is asking me to take to realize the power of the gospel more fully in my life? How could this impact my children?

CHAPTER SEVEN

# SAVORING THE PRECIOUS MOMENTS

*Building Meaningful Relationships with Your Kids*

*Admonish the young women to . . . love their children.*

TITUS 2:4

EVERY NIGHT AS Eric and I are drifting off to sleep, we have a little tradition. He says, "Remember the kiddos?" which prompts me to recount several funny, quirky, and/or adorable things our little "pumpkin doodles" did that day, such as little Kip telling me that he had the "peacocks," which meant he had the hiccups. He also told the babysitter that he had a "mustache" on his arm, which meant he had a rash. (We are still working on his vocabulary skills, but for now it's entertaining to hear what he comes up with.) Or Hudson setting up "Hudson's Toy Store" in his bedroom and doing a high-pressure sales job on every unsuspecting person who enters our home, selling random articles from around the house at a premium price. There was a great sale going on today though; I got a pair of swim trunks, a baby hair bow, and a well-used book—all for seventy-five cents.

Such anecdotes are precious to Mommy's and Daddy's hearts. But in the bustle of daily life, we forget these priceless moments unless we take the time to savor and enjoy them. Our nightly tradition cultivates a deeper tenderness and appreciation for the children God has given us and refreshes our perspective as parents. Instead of focusing on the challenges of parenting or on a discipline issue, we remember that these munchkins truly are a blessing from the hand of God, not just a duty or responsibility.

I've discovered that the best way for me to savor the joy and beauty of motherhood is to nurture my relationships with my children throughout the day. This sometimes requires putting my to-do list on hold while I listen to their little speeches, show enthusiasm for their new discoveries and accomplishments, take time to examine and admire a roly-poly with them, or chase them around the backyard while they giggle hysterically. Training, discipline, routine, and structure are important, but these things are tools that enable me to focus on what matters in motherhood: building healthy relationships with my children and leading them to Jesus Christ.

It's all too easy to get so caught up in the logistics of managing our homes and disciplining our children that we forget to enjoy our children. I remember hearing a time-management message from a homeschooling mother of seven. It was filled with helpful information, from how to manage the laundry to keeping kids on track with their schoolwork throughout the day. This particular mom was diligent about rising early in the morning, structuring the flow of her children's day, having regular mealtimes with the family, and making sure all household chores were accomplished. She shared the wisdom and practical tips she'd learned, and for the most part her home seemed to run like clockwork. But when asked if she ever spent one-on-one time building relationships with her children, she replied, "Very little! I just don't have time for that with everything else I'm doing."

It made me sad to hear that response. As discussed in previous chapters, I'm a fan of order, structure, and discipline in the home. But I don't believe those things should ever become our end goal. Rather, they simply help enable a mother to spend time on what truly matters. Titus 2:4-5 says, "Admonish the young women to love their husbands, to love their children, to be discreet, chaste, homemakers. . . ." Becoming an excellent homemaker is of great importance in God's eyes, but it's not at the top of the list—loving my husband and children must come first.

We can show love to our spouses and kids by tending to their practical needs, making our homes into sanctuaries, and building a stable routine for them. But we must also show love to them by spending purposeful time with them, becoming a trusted depository for their hopes, dreams, and struggles, and appreciating the unique people they are becoming.

This is not an easy balance to find. My biggest challenge in life is managing our home and ministry well while also spending purposeful time with my children. I'm constantly asking

God for wisdom in how to be excellent in both areas. When it comes to motherhood, it would be easy for me to spend my time organizing, planning, scheduling, and cleaning rather than playing, laughing, and making memories with my kids.

But I don't want to look back in twenty years and remember an organized home devoid of meaningful family relationships. I don't want my kids to remember me as a mom who kept an orderly household but never had time for them. So each week, I try to be intentional about making memories with my kids.

For instance, not long ago we had "bubble day." I filled up our water table with bubble solution and let the kids use straws and bubble wands to make all shapes and sizes of bubbles. I made chocolate milk and let them blow bubbles in it (a special one-time privilege). We read about the science of bubbles. We did a bubble art project involving bubble solution and colored tempura paint. Yes, it was a mess, but it was worth it for the fun we had. Last, I put bubble wrap on the floor and let the kids jump on it and pop the bubbles. These activities were simple and inexpensive, but the memories we made together will last for many years to come.

One day not long ago the crisp fall weather was particularly beautiful, so I decided to load all four kids into the car and take them to the local pumpkin patch. We jumped on hay bales, took an inordinately long and bumpy wagon ride, fed some sheep and a fat pig, and collected a variety of pumpkins and gourds to decorate and bake with. When we got home, I let the kids go to town beautifying their pumpkins with stickers, glitter, and markers.

These were simple, inexpensive activities. And yet, their impact upon my relationship with my kids was truly invaluable.

I certainly do not have it all figured out when it comes to making memories or building relational time with my kids into every day. Like most moms, I often struggle with the feeling that I should be doing more than I am. But I know that God has placed this burden upon my heart for a very important reason. By His grace, I intend to make the most of every moment that I can during these precious years of my children's lives.

## MAKING IT PRACTICAL

Here are two principles that have helped me build meaningful relationships with my children.

### 1. DELIGHT IN YOUR KIDS

Everyone is always telling me how fast kids grow up. But I believe that if we slow down and savor the moments we have with our children every day, we will not one day feel like the years with them passed us by, because we took time to treasure and enjoy them.

Sometimes we as mothers can become so busy and overwhelmed that we overlook the built-in "laughter therapy" that God has given us right in our own families. When I am juggling a lot of tasks, discipline issues, and responsibilities, it is easy to not take time to delight in my kids. But kids are hilarious. They say funny and precious things nearly every day.

One of the ways to appreciate these moments is to listen when children are talking, instead of just "zoning out" and responding with a distracted "uh huh." This is much easier said than done. Often in our home four little voices chatter at once. I try to make a habit of getting eye-level with my kids whenever they are trying to tell me something specific, such as a detailed description of their playtime antics or a funny dream they had. Looking them in the eye helps me focus on what they are saying and shows them that I value their thoughts and ideas. It helps me pay attention and take time to notice the cute and quirky statements that come out of their mouths and the way their little personalities are developing.

Of course, it's not always practical to get down on their level, look them in the eye, and listen intently to our kids. But as much as possible, I try to pay attention when they talk, respond with enthusiasm and interest, ask questions, and take delight in their thoughts, ideas, and accomplishments.

Whenever one of our kids says something funny or unique, I try to write it down on my computer before I forget it. Then during our nightly ritual of remembering the kiddos, I recount these things to Eric so we can both get a good chuckle out of them.

I also love making digital photo albums of our kids. I'm not a professional photographer by any means, and I'm not especially artistic. However, I'm blessed with some wonderful photographer friends who graciously take lots of pictures of our kids. Modern technology makes it easy for me to create simple and beautiful digital photo books using templates.

Our coffee table is adorned with photo books of family activities, memories, and milestones in our children's lives. I like to sit down with my kids and flip through these special memories every so often. It reminds me how much of a treasure my children are.

Remember that God hasn't given you children merely for the purpose of training and disciplining them, but also so you can enjoy them and delight in them. Taking time to appreciate the uniqueness of your children will help them feel even more special and loved, and it will add a refreshing splash of humor and sparkle to your motherhood role.

## 2. PLAN FAMILY ACTIVITIES AHEAD

I find it challenging to think of creative, memory-building family activities on the spot. If I wait until Saturday morning to come up with something enjoyable for our family to do that weekend, I use up half of our "family fun day" just trying to figure out something fun to do. The same is true for family nights during the week. There are so many potential distractions and tasks during any given week that if I don't plan our family time in advance, it typically falls through the cracks.

I try to set aside time each weekend to map out several special family activities for the coming week. I may also make a trip to the store for any materials that might be needed (such as art and craft supplies or treat-baking materials). Recently, I started a "family fun" notebook to help me out when I need inspiration. Anytime I see an article or flyer that gives me a great idea for something we can do together as a family, I add it to the notebook. It's so much easier to flip open to pages of ideas, directions, costs, and inspirational photos than to sit staring blankly out the window trying to think of something creative for our family to do together.

Many great books, websites, and resources offer fun and creative ideas you can do with your children. I'm fond of browsing through preschool and elementary teacher's books or party planning books to come up with fun themes for art projects, games, and field trips. (For some of my favorites, see the recommended resources on page 157.)

Remember that time with your family doesn't need to be elaborate or expensive to be meaningful. Your children will feel valued and loved knowing that you set aside time just to focus on being with them.

The other day I took my girls to a craft store and let them pick out a simple art project. Then we took the material to a nearby bakery and worked on creating a "masterpiece" while enjoying the rare privilege of eating a frosted doughnut. The excursion took about an hour and didn't cost much. But the girls talked about it for days afterward.

A hike in the woods or a rock-skipping session at a nearby lake can become a memory that will last a lifetime. So can a cup of hot chocolate and a story on the couch. You don't need a trip to Disneyland to create precious memories with your children. What your kids want most of all is thoughtful, focused, and purposeful time with you.

Not long ago our family was in a restaurant, and Eric and I were helping each of the kids color while we waited for our food. The waitress commented how unusual it was to see a family doing something together while eating out. "Normally Mom and Dad are texting or checking e-mail on their phones, and the kids are playing games on iPads. Families don't talk to each other anymore," she told us sadly.

How easy it is in our modern age to be around our kids and not really be with them! I've been guilty many times of checking my phone when I should have been engaging with my children. Positive memories are not made when we merely spend time *around* our kids but when we *focus* on them. So ask your kids questions, listen to their stories, and engage in conversation as you spend time together. (And turn off your phone if it helps you focus better!)

When you look back on the years you shared with your family, you will not remember the way your pantry was organized or the smoothness of your morning routine. What will stand out are the memories that were made when you took the time to cultivate relationships with your children.

## LET'S TALK ABOUT IT

*Group Study and Discussion*

1. **Read Malachi 4:6.** What causes parents' hearts to turn toward their children? What is the difference between Christ-centered love between parents and

children, and the natural human family affection that even non-Christians demonstrate?

2. **Read Titus 2:4-5.** What are some of the most effective ways you have shown love to your kids by building meaningful relationships with them? What has been the impact of those decisions?

3. **Read Luke 8:14.** What are some of the most common distractions that keep us from cherishing and appreciating our children? How can we keep these distractions at bay?

## TAKE IT DEEPER

*Personal Study and Reflection*

**Read:** Luke 10:40

**Reflect:** Am I neglecting things that are truly important—such as spending time with my children—because I'm distracted by worries and daily tasks? If so, how might God be asking me to change these patterns?

**Read:** Proverbs 31:28

**Reflect:** What have been the most meaningful memories I've made with my children? What made them so effective?

**Read:** Luke 21:34

**Reflect:** What are the biggest threats to my ability to build lasting relationships with my children? How can I protect my family from these threats?

# PART THREE

# MOTHERING WITH STRENGTH AND DIGNITY

*Truth and Encouragement for the Daily Challenges of Motherhood*

# CHAPTER EIGHT

# PRAYERFUL MOTHERING

*Parenting with the Weapons of Heaven*

*Be anxious for nothing, but in everything by prayer and supplication,*
*with thanksgiving, let your requests be made known to God.*

PHILIPPIANS 4:6

OUR SON HUDSON IS named after one of our spiritual heroes—the great missionary to China, Hudson Taylor—because we desire that our son follow in his footsteps of tenacious faith and unwavering devotion to Christ. But years before Hudson Taylor became the father of evangelical missions, he was a wayward teen with no interest in God. Burdened for the salvation of her son, his mother labored diligently in prayer on his behalf, asking God to rescue his soul. One day, when she was away from home, staying with a friend, she felt pressed to wrestle in prayer for Hudson. She knelt by her bed and determined not to rise from the spot until she was confident that her son's soul had been won for

Christ. Hour after hour she pleaded for Hudson, until at last she knew in her heart that the victory had been gained. Christ's Spirit made it clear to her that her son had come into the kingdom of God that very day.

When she arrived home several days later, Hudson met her at the door to tell her the joyful news that he had given his life to Christ, and she realized it was on the same afternoon she had wrestled for him in prayer. The tireless prayers of this faithful mother helped shape one of the greatest spiritual heroes this world has ever known, leading to the salvation of countless souls and giving thousands a heart and passion for foreign missions.[10]

We can change the world through faithfully praying for our children. Countless mothers, like Hudson Taylor's, already have. But we cannot fight large-scale battles in prayer until we have practiced on the small, everyday challenges we face in raising our children. God's Word exhorts us to "pray without ceasing" (1 Thess. 5:17), and being a mother provides plenty of opportunities to pray daily, hourly, and moment by moment. It might seem silly to pray about mundane child-raising issues such as potty training, pacifier weaning, table manners, and sleep patterns. But such prayers strengthen our prayer muscles. ☺

If we pray about everything, knowing that God cares about every detail of our lives (see Mt. 10:30), we will begin to notice His faithfulness day by day. As a result, we will be made strong in faith and spiritually ready for the bigger battles ahead.

When our adopted daughter Harper first came home from Korea as a baby, we experienced many challenges as she transitioned into our home. While still in Korea, Harper had been diagnosed with "stranger anxiety," and the social worker was concerned about her ability to bond with us. I envisioned the agony of having a child who would scream every time I tried to comfort her or cuddle with her. But Eric and I committed together to ask God to remove all Harper's stranger anxiety before she even came home, and God answered our prayer in a miraculous way. From the moment we held her, Harper seemed to know that we were her parents. When the social worker came to check on her the day after her arrival, she was shocked at how well Harper had bonded with us and how happy she seemed. We knew it was a direct answer to our prayers.

Seeing God's faithfulness in this area inspired us to pray faithfully for every issue—small or big—that we faced in parenting our new little daughter. Harper had never slept in a crib before, and her sleep schedule was opposite of ours since she came from the other side of the world. Her car seat terrified her. So I began praying over Harper nearly every moment of the day. *Lord, I pray that she would feel totally comfortable in her car seat. Lord, may she sleep through the night without any interruptions. Lord, may Harper's nap schedule line up perfectly with Hudson's.*

The answers didn't always come instantly, but they did come. Harper's adjustment into a new country, new family, and new life was truly supernatural. Other women would sometimes ask me what we did to help Harper transition into our family so smoothly. The only answer I could give was, "We prayed!"

Some moms would get disgruntled with that answer. "Well, yes, but I mean—besides that," they would counter, wanting something more practical from me. Sure, there were a few functional things we did to help Harper adjust to her crib and car seat, but I am convinced that prayer was the primary reason behind every success we achieved. As moms, we are so eager for practical solutions to the everyday challenges we face with our children that we can forget about our biggest, most powerful parenting weapon: prayer. Prayer shouldn't be an afterthought; it should be the bedrock of our child rearing. Anything practical we do should be an outflow of our faithful, diligent prayers for each detail of our children's lives.

Hudson Taylor's mother could have sought out practical solutions to help her rebellious, apathetic son. She could have searched for the right book to give him, the right church to drag him to, or the right mentor to disciple him. But Mrs. Taylor knew that until she had truly petitioned heaven on behalf of her son, everything she tried would just be a human solution to a God-sized problem. Wrestling in prayer for Hudson was the most powerful, effective way to reach his soul, and she knew it.

When Kipling was about three, Eric and I noticed that during playtime he often pretended to be a "bad guy." So, we started praying that he would catch a vision for being a protector, not a villain. Not long after we began to pray about this, our son's attitude changed. I still remember him running happily outside to play while announcing, "Mommy, I'm a hero, not a bad guy!"

Never forget: God cares more about your children than even you do. You can entrust every issue, big or small, into His faithful hands. If you learn how to win small victories in prayer now, you will be ready for the more significant battles that lie ahead, battles that affect the generations to come.

Whether you are wrestling in prayer over potty training your toddler or laboring over the fate of your child's eternal soul, the victory lies in wrestling, importunate, diligent prayer.

The old hymn "What a Friend We Have in Jesus" beautifully captures the heart attitude of a prayerful mother:

> What a friend we have in Jesus; all our sins and griefs
>> to bear!
> What a privilege to carry everything to God in prayer!
> O what peace we often forfeit, O what needless pain
>> we bear,
> All because we do not carry everything to God in
>> prayer.
> Have we trials and temptations? Is there trouble
>> anywhere?
> We should never be discouraged; take it to the Lord
>> in prayer!

Can we find a friend so faithful who will all our
    sorrows share?
Jesus knows our every weakness; take it to the Lord
    in prayer.

## BECOMING A FAITH-FILLED MOTHER

Mary Slessor, a missionary to West Africa in the 1800s, once
wrote about the significant role prayer played in her ministry.
She said,

> My life is one long daily, hourly record of answered
> prayer. For physical health, for mental overstrain, for
> guidance given marvelously, for errors and dangers
> averted, for enmity to the Gospel subdued, for food
> provided at the exact hour needed, for everything
> that goes to make up life and my poor service, I can
> testify with a full and often wonder-stricken awe
> that I believe God answers prayer.[11]

Imagine if we had the faith to not just hope but to *know* that
God will provide for every need or challenge we may face in
our mothering. If prayer is just wishful thinking or spiritual-
sounding chitchat, it will accomplish nothing in our lives.
But if we pray with a heart of childlike faith in a God who
can never fail, our prayers will accomplish mighty things.

    Here are a few steps that have most helped me become
stronger in my faith, and thus, in my prayer life:

## 1. FIND STORIES THAT BUILD FAITH

Surround yourself with believers who are strong in faith, Christians who believe that God is as big as He claims to be and have seen His power and faithfulness demonstrated in mighty ways. When I listen to firsthand accounts of God's faithfulness in other people's lives, I recognize my own low expectations of God, and as a result, I pray bigger prayers and see more miraculous things happen in *my* everyday life.

Historical accounts of great Christians throughout the ages have also inspired me toward a life of faith. History is filled with stories of mighty men and women who overcame impossible obstacles through faith in the power of their God. The problem is, in our modern day and age, we don't hear many stories that build our faith. Rather, we seem to hear the opposite. Many authors of popular Christian books talk candidly about their disappointment with God, their difficulty finding a real experience with God, and their grappling with the reality that God just doesn't seem as big as Scripture makes Him out to be.

Such messages don't build faith. To grow in faith, we must flood our hearts, minds, and souls with reminders of the faithfulness and power of our God—and disregard all messages that speak anything else.

In Ephesians 1:19, Paul writes that he desires us to grasp "the exceeding greatness of His power toward us who believe, according to the working of His mighty power." God has provided mighty power for His children; He has called us to perform valiant exploits for His kingdom and His glory.

But this power can only be accessed by those who believe. If you find it difficult to grasp the greatness of God's power, begin listening to testimonies about His faithfulness. If you know heroic Christians who have witnessed the power of God, meet with them and ask them to tell you their stories.

Even if you don't know any faith-filled Christians, plenty of inspiring books and biographies contain the testimonies of mighty men and women of God who have gone before you. Here are some of my favorites:

- *Chasing the Dragon* by Jackie Pullinger (Ventura, CA: Regal Books/Gospel Light, 1980)

- *George Mueller of Bristol* by George Mueller (Old Tappan, NJ: Fleming H. Revel, 1899)

- *Gold Cord* by Amy Carmichael (Fort Washington, PA: CLC Publications, 1991)

- *Hudson Taylor's Spiritual Secret* by Dr. and Mrs. Howard Taylor (Chicago, IL: Moody Publishers, 2009)

- *Oswald Chambers: Abandoned to God* by David McCasland (Grand Rapids, MI: Discovery House Publishers, 1993)

- *Rees Howells: Intercessor* by Norman Grubb (Fort Washington, PA: CLC Publications, 1988)

- *The Pastor's Wife* by Sabina Wurmbrand (London, England: Hodder and Stoughton, 1970)

- *Tramp for the Lord* by Corrie ten Boom (Fort Washington, PA: CLC Publications, 2008)

## 2. STUDY THE ART OF TRUE PRAYER

To strengthen your prayer muscles, read Christian books that take the Word of God seriously and exhort you to expect big things of God. Eric and I have noticed that when we read faith-building books just before our prayer times, we are much more inspired and motivated to wrestle in prayer until the battle is won. Here are a few that have most inspired me:

- *The Complete Works of E. M. Bounds on Prayer* (Radford, VA: Wilder Publications, 2009)

- *Revival Praying* by Leonard Ravenhill (Ada, MI: Bethany House, 2005)

- *Why Revival Tarries* by Leonard Ravenhill (Ada, MI: Bethany House, 2004)

Eric and I have also written a book called *Wrestling Prayer* (Eugene, OR: Harvest House, 2009), which details our personal journey to develop a powerful and effective prayer life.

## 3. KEEP A PRAYER JOURNAL—AND GET SPECIFIC

Many Christian young people have said to Eric and me, "I never pray for anything specific. I've always been told that if you pray for something specific and God doesn't answer it, you'll get disillusioned with God." This is a typical attitude among modern Christians. We are afraid to get too specific with our praying, because we are worried that God won't answer us. It's far easier to pray vague, general prayers so we don't get our hopes disappointed.

But Christ asks us to pray specific prayers. It's the pattern of Scripture. (See Mt. 21:22; Phil. 4:6; and 1 Jn. 5:14, as examples.) And when we go out on a limb and make a specific request of God, our faith grows as we see Him come through for us.

Are you having specific discipline issues with one of your children? Challenges getting everyone out the door on time in the morning? Difficulty staying organized? Worried about your children making the right friends? Concerned over your child's lack of spiritual hunger? Take it to God in specific, importunate prayer! No matter how small or big the issue is, nothing falls outside His desire and ability to assist His children.

One of the best ways to build your faith is to begin a prayer journal and write down your detailed requests. Then wrestle in prayer for them on a daily basis until the breakthrough comes. Record every answer to prayer, small or large, in your journal. Then, a few months or years later, you'll be able to read back over your prayer journal and see God's faithfulness. Whenever I've kept a prayer journal and revisited it later on, I'm always amazed at how God demonstrated His power in my life, and my faith is built mighty and strong.

Eric and I have found that we didn't understand praying until we began to pray specifically. As Charles Spurgeon said, "There is a general kind of praying which fails for lack of precision. It is as if a regiment of soldiers should all fire off their guns anywhere. Possibly somebody would be killed, but the majority of the enemy would be missed."[12]

✳   ✳   ✳

No matter what challenge we face in our parenting, if we as mothers put these words into action, we will begin to see miracles in our children's lives. Jesus sees every sparrow that falls, He knows the number of hairs on our children's heads, and He cares about them more than we can imagine. No issue is ever too small or too big to take to our God in prayer.

## LET'S TALK ABOUT IT

### Group Study and Discussion

1. **Read Philippians 4:6.** Why do we often turn to anxiety instead of prayer when it comes to issues our children are facing? How would our families change for the better if we began praying diligently about every challenge we face as mothers?

2. **Read Luke 1:37.** What are some of the most significant answers to prayer you have seen as a parent? How did these experiences strengthen your family's faith in God?

3. **Read Matthew 26:41.** What are some of the biggest hindrances to building a consistent prayer life? What are some ways we as mothers can make prayer a higher priority in our homes?

## TAKE IT DEEPER

### *Personal Study and Reflection*

**Read:** 1 Peter 5:7

**Reflect:** Do I habitually cast my cares upon Christ? Do I trust that He cares about my children and that He hears and answers my prayers on their behalf?

**Read:** Isaiah 25:1

**Reflect:** In what specific ways have I witnessed God's faithfulness to me as a mother? What are the most significant prayers He's answered? Do I trust that He will continue to be faithful to me and my family?

**Read:** Ephesians 6:18

**Reflect:** How can I make prayer a greater priority in my daily life? What are some steps God might be asking me to take in order to build my faith stronger?

# CHAPTER NINE

# FEARLESS MOTHERHOOD

*Entrusting Your Children to the Creator's Care*

*She is not afraid of snow for her household, for all her household is clothed
with scarlet.*

PROVERBS 31:21

HERE IN COLORADO, I'm surrounded by thrill seekers—
people who love to scale steep mountain cliffs during light-
ning storms or hang over dropoffs forty feet above the ground,
suspended only by a thin rope. My two younger brothers
enjoy bungee jumping off high cliffs, ice climbing up slippery embankments with pickaxes, and off-trail-double-black-
diamond skiing through avalanche country. They have some
great stories to share from their many adventures.

I've always been more of a play-it-safe kind of girl. It's not
that I'm a wimp; I'm just not a big risk-taker. I don't enjoy
the adrenaline rush that comes with defying death on the side
of a mountain. To quote Marilla Cuthbert (from the movie

*Anne of Green Gables*): "I'd rather walk calmly along, and do without flying *and* thud." Yet motherhood is filled with opportunities to fret, fear, worry, panic, and experience far bigger adrenaline rushes than any extreme mountaineering adventure could ever provide.

Eric and I have worked hard to make our home safe for our children, with locks on medicine cabinets and barricades on tool drawers. However, kids have a knack for finding the one moment when something potentially dangerous is sitting out on the counter for two minutes. When Avonlea was two, she found a bottle of natural cough syrup on the bathroom counter and told me she drank it. While it was more likely that she dumped it down the sink, I still felt a little panicky. After being on the phone with poison control for thirty minutes, I was relieved to discover that this particular syrup was nontoxic. And I can't forget the time a couple of months ago that Hudson ran into our bedroom at 3 a.m. announcing that Kip had vanished in the night. We searched the house for what felt like an eternity (it was actually just a few minutes) before we finally found him fast asleep underneath his bunk bed.

From charging straight toward the deep end of the swimming pool without a life vest to jumping from the highest point of the playground's climbing wall, my children know how to push their mother's "panic button." No matter how watchful I am, they always try a new death-defying feat during that one moment when my back is turned. And I know I'm not alone in my "mommy adrenaline rush" moments.

Whenever I'm at the park or pool around other moms, I frequently hear such statements as, "You almost gave me a heart attack!" or "What are you trying to do—get yourself killed?!"

God has given mothers a fierce protectiveness over our children. Most of us would gladly sacrifice our own well-being to make sure that our little ones are kept healthy and safe. But all too often, the Enemy of our soul and the warped culture in which we live attempt to twist this natural God-given protectiveness into an attitude of paranoia and fear.

"You're a mother; you can't help but worry!" is a comment I've heard from many fellow moms. It's common to believe that having children is a good excuse for living in fear and worrying constantly about all the things that might happen to them. And yet, when God commands us to "fear not" (Is. 41:10), He doesn't say, "except when it comes to your children." Rather, He commands us to be strong and courageous in *all* areas of life, including motherhood. We are walking according to His pattern when we "are not afraid with any terror" (1 Pet. 3:6).

I realize this is far easier said than done. Just like every other "mama bear" out there, I understand well the temptation toward fretting and paranoia over our children's health and safety. When my kids get sick or hurt, I'm tempted to ponder the worst-case scenario. *What if they end up in the hospital? What if this is really serious?* On and on the worries roll like tumultuous ocean waves. If I allow those thoughts and suggestions to take root, I become paralyzed by dread and panic, the very things God asks me not to allow into my life.

But when I turn to Him for strength, He enables me to walk a different path: to choose faith instead of fear and to entrust my children into His more-than-capable, ever-faithful arms of protection and love. When fear knocks, He reminds me that He cares more about my children than I ever could, that He wants the very best for them, and that He has promised to faithfully watch over them like a loving Shepherd. He is a far better protector than I ever could be.

Contrary to popular belief, our job as mothers is not to fret, worry, and imagine the worst-case scenario. God has called us to fearless motherhood. We are to bring "every thought into captivity to the obedience of Christ" (2 Cor. 10:5) and not allow fear to have dominion over us. We are not to obsess over every new study in child safety or panic about every germ that comes near our kids. Worrying doesn't accomplish anything of value and only brings turmoil into our lives (see Mt. 6:27). But resting securely in God's faithful and loving care brings perfect peace to our souls (see Is. 26:3).

Yes, there will always be those momentary surges of adrenaline when our children startle us with their new and daring feats. And yes, we still need to use our God-given protection radar and keep a watchful eye over our children's well-being. But by God's grace, may we not dishonor Him by wallowing in fear, lying awake fretting over all the terrible things that could possibly happen to our children. Rather, like the Proverbs 31 woman, may we have no fear for our household, for our children are clothed in scarlet, covered

*Love this idea*

by the precious blood of our King. May we fully entrust our children to His faithful, loving, watchful care.

## HANDLING THE "WHAT IFS"

Many of us have been plagued by fretful "what if" scenarios regarding our kids. *What if they get sick? What if they get hurt? What if they get mistreated by other kids? What if they don't make good grades? What if they have emotional problems? What if they don't reach their full potential?* And the list goes on and on.

As we trust in God's protection, we can rest confidently in the fact that the Enemy cannot "have his way" with our children (see Lk. 10:19; Jas. 4:7). Yet this doesn't mean that God will never allow our children to face difficulties or that we as Christian mothers won't walk through "trials of many kinds" involving our children (Jas. 1:2, NIV).

So how can we keep those "what ifs" from ruling our thoughts and emotions, turning us into fretting, paranoid, worrywarts? How do we know we'll be able to handle difficult circumstances if and when they come?

In her book *The Hiding Place*, Corrie ten Boom shares a story from her childhood when she told her father about her fear of facing hardship and suffering:

"Corrie," he began gently. "When you and I go to Amsterdam—when do I give you your ticket?" . . .

"Why, just before we get on the train."

119

"Exactly. And our wise Father in heaven knows when we're going to need things, too. Don't run out ahead of Him, Corrie. When the time comes [for you to suffer], you will look into your heart and find the strength you need—just in time."[13]

Fretting and worrying about "what ifs" shows a lack of trust in our God. We envision all the possible trials we might face, but we fail to look at them through a heavenly lens and remember the grace, strength, and victory that God offers for every challenge we must walk through. We must remember that God gives us the grace we need for specific trials right when we need it—and not before.

Rather than worrying about what might happen in the future, we can rest securely in this knowledge:

God can turn anything the Enemy means for evil into good in our lives (see Gen. 50:20; Ro. 8:28).

He will not allow us to walk through trials we are not able to handle (see 1 Cor. 10:13).

Even when we walk through difficult circumstances, we can triumph through every challenge when we put our hope in Him (see Ps. 25:3).

Worrying about "what ifs" is not only dangerous to our spiritual lives, but it also distracts us from "being all there" for our children. Elisabeth Elliot wrote,

Worry is refusing the given. Today's care, not tomorrow's, is the responsibility given to us, apportioned in the wisdom of God. Often we neglect the thing assigned for the moment because we are preoccupied with something that is not our business just now. How easy it is to give only half our attention to someone who needs us—friend, husband, or little child—because the other half is focused on a future worry.[14]

Whenever you are tempted to dwell on fearful "what if" scenarios, take a moment to deliberately fill your mind with Truth. A great way to start applying this principle is by memorizing some of the Psalms. (Some of my favorites on this subject are Psalm 27, 34, 37, 46, 91, and 112.) Whenever you are faced with the temptation to fear, those words of Truth can become vital weapons with which you chase away foreboding, anxious thoughts. The more you consistently fill your mind with Truth, the scarcer the Enemy's lies will become.

Another great principle is to pray for someone whenever fearful thoughts attempt to enter your mind. Praying for someone else takes your focus off yourself and your own fears—and turns you outward instead of inward.

When we truly know our God and believe Him to be exactly as His Word says He is, we have no reason to let fearful thoughts overtake our minds, because we know that in every situation, no matter how difficult, He will show Himself faithful.

## TRUSTING GOD IN THE HELPLESS MOMENTS

It was a cold January evening. The roads were icy. Snow was coming down in torrents. I had just finished packing for a two-week family vacation to sunny California. The car was loaded, and I was looking forward to crawling into bed after a long day of laboring through eleven loads of laundry and cramming swim vests, floaty toys, princess dresses, and Legos into overfilled suitcases. Around 9 p.m., five-year-old Harper came running into the kitchen. "I don't feel good," she whimpered, holding her chest. Assuming she must be dealing with some kind of indigestion, I had her drink some water and searched the vitamin cabinet for some kind of tummy-aid. She continued crying and carrying on inconsolably for ten or fifteen minutes. No amount of comfort or physical help seemed to be working.

Finally, she admitted the truth. "I swallowed a penny. It's stuck in my chest." Of course, I had a lovely lecture on the tip of my tongue, along the lines of, "Um, exactly *how* did you get a penny at nine o' clock at night? Weren't you supposed to be in bed? And why in the world did you put that penny in your mouth and swallow it? You are way too old to be doing such a thing!"

But now was not the time for an inquisition. I could get the details later. Since Eric was not feeling well that night, we decided he would stay with the kids, and I would take Harper to the emergency room. I bundled her up, and we headed out into the cold night air, praying all the way, not only for Harper's health but also for our safety through the hazardous driving conditions. It was well below zero outside. The roads were slippery, and the visibility was poor. We finally made it to the hospital with the help of my dad, who met us en route and took over the driving.

I assumed that when we got to the ER, they would give Harper some kind of special drink to make the penny slippery enough to go down into her stomach. I didn't expect it to be a big ordeal, just a minor inconvenience. Well, not only did it turn out to be an ordeal, it was also one of the scariest and most miserable nights of my life. After getting X-rays taken and waiting for two hours, we finally saw the physician, who told us we needed to transfer Harper to another hospital where they could do a special "procedure" to get the penny out.

So we bundled up again and headed across town on the slippery roads. The next hospital was crowded and stressful. We were in a semiprivate room shared by about twenty other people, with only a curtain to shield us from the disconcerting sounds of the injured and ill a few feet away. That was when I started to feel my adrenaline pumping. I texted Eric, who informed me that he was flat on his back in misery with a severe stomach flu. He could hardly move, let alone get up and come to the hospital. My parents were there to lend their support, but it was going to be up to me to make all the decisions. My knees started feeling a little weak. Inwardly I reminded myself of Christ's promise, "I will never leave you nor forsake you," (Heb. 13:5) and recited the words over and over in my mind.

After another set of X-rays and another long wait, the new physician told me that Harper needed to have emergency surgery. Not exactly the simple "procedure" I'd envisioned, where I could sit right by her side and hold her hand as they gently guided the coin down into her tummy. Rather, they would put her completely under and take her to the operating room. They would put her on a breathing tube and insert a scope down her throat and into her chest. They assured me it was a safe process but meanwhile asked me to sign a legal form that said I understood all the risks of such a surgery. I couldn't even bring myself to read the list of possible dangers. They had called a specialist surgeon to come to the hospital, and he came bustling into the room still in his jeans, hat, and jacket, hurriedly telling me he would get into his scrubs and meet me upstairs to prep her for surgery. Everything was happening quickly and urgently.

I was scared. Really scared. It didn't help to hear the nurse say, "This is a routine surgery; lots of other kids swallow coins too!" This wasn't any other kid. It was Harper, my precious little treasure whom I'd nurtured and cared for since she was a tiny baby. She seemed so little and helpless as they put an IV into her arm. I had only a few moments to kiss her, pray for her, and reassure her before they wheeled her into surgery in a rolling hospital bed. They promised it would be quick and that I should hear an update within thirty minutes or so. An hour went by, and there was no word at all. I was pacing the waiting room floor, praying a mile a minute, and crying out to God for help. It was probably the longest hour of my life. I was in agony, wanting to know that Harper was okay but unable to hear any news.

The nurse finally came in to say it was taking longer than they expected, because instead of pulling the penny up into her throat, they had inadvertently pushed it down, most likely into her tummy. They had to find an X-ray specialist in order to take another picture and ensure that the coin was indeed in her tummy and not in her lungs or another risky location. They had given her more anesthesia, and she was still on a breathing tube, because they could not wake her up until they knew for sure where the penny was.

At this point, it was nearly 3 a.m., and this ordeal had been going on for six hours. Eric was extremely ill and could only text a word or two at a time. I felt so helpless. There was nothing I could do practically to help my daughter. All I could do was cry out to God for His divine intervention.

Whenever I've faced a scary storm cloud in my mothering, I have had two options. I can pay attention to the fear, the "what ifs," and focus on the wind and rain raging all around me. This choice always leads to utter despair. Or, I can choose instead to dwell upon the faithfulness and promises of God and surrender to His loving control over every situation. And even though I might feel the emotions of fear or desperation, He has given me the power to take those thoughts and feelings captive, instead of allowing them to rule me.

So at that moment, I called upon God to bring my

tumultuous emotions under His control. I began to meditate upon His faithfulness in my life, especially all the supernatural ways He had worked in Harper's little life. Though my heart was racing and my knees were still a bit weak, as I continued to pray, I slowly gained an assurance in my heart that Harper would be okay. I reminded myself that even though I was helpless in that moment, He was certainly not.

The nurse looked at me and said, "Don't worry, honey, you are doing well. Most mothers would be lying on the floor in hysterics right about now."

Even though I didn't feel strong or resilient, I realized that her observation was the evidence of God's grace in me. Though my emotions were in agony, my spirit began to trust that He was in control and that He would be faithful.

For the next forty-five minutes as I again waited for word on how Harper was doing, I repeatedly commanded my emotions to line up with my soul's declaration: *I will not fear; my God is in control; He will never leave me or forsake me.*

Yes, the adrenaline and concern were still present. But I determined I would not allow panic or despair to set in. My focus *had* to remain on God and not on my circumstances. The moment I started looking at the wind and rain, and not at Him, I knew I would begin to sink, just like Peter had, when attempting to walk on the water.

Finally, the surgeon came out to tell us that the penny had landed safely in Harper's tummy, and they were waking her up from the anesthesia. I began to rejoice in God's faithfulness. Yet, it wasn't until they allowed me to see her about an hour later that my heart began to beat normally again. There she was, sleeping safely and peacefully, sporting a large gap where her loose front tooth had been knocked out during surgery. The words of Psalm 34:4 began resounding through my soul: "I sought the LORD, and He heard me, and delivered me from all my fears."

Oh, what a trustworthy God we serve!

A week or two after the hospital visit, I got Harper's surgery bill in the mail. It cost over twelve thousand dollars to remove the penny she swallowed. A one-cent coin had somehow turned into a twelve-thousand-dollar ordeal! But the spiritual reminder God gave me that night was truly invaluable.

As a parent, I am not capable of protecting my children from all danger. There will be moments in my mothering journey when I will feel helpless to take away their pain, when I will desperately want to remove them from harm's way and yet be unable to do so. But even when all I can do is cry out to God for protection, help, and deliverance, *I am not helpless*. Because He is not helpless. He loves and cherishes my children. And He will never leave or forsake them, or me.

Though I'm not a huge fan of Harper's superexpensive penny, or the hospital bills that followed, I do believe it was worth twelve thousand dollars to learn the lesson of God's faithfulness firsthand. Let us never forget that His love for our children begins where our comprehension ends. Whatever difficult trials we may face as mothers, there is an abundance of grace to walk through every hardship with triumph and courage when God is our rock (see Ps. 62:2).

## LET'S TALK ABOUT IT

*Group Study and Discussion*

1. **Read Matthew 6:27-34.** What is God's solution for gaining victory over fear and having a heart and mind guarded by peace?

2. **Read Psalm 37:8.** Why is fretting and worrying destructive to our family life and our own souls? How do we gain the strength to replace worry with faith?

3. **Read Proverbs 31:25 and 1 Peter 3:6.** Have you ever observed a mother who exuded these qualities of childlike confidence in God? What did you notice about her life and her family?

## TAKE IT DEEPER

*Personal Study and Reflection*

**Read:** Deuteronomy 31:6, NIV

**Reflect:** Do I think of myself as a victim of fear? What spiritual or practical steps is God asking me to take in order to obey His command to "be strong and courageous"?

**Read:** Psalm 91

**Reflect:** Do I believe these promises are for my family? Am I entrusting my children to God's care, or am I fearfully trying to do His job for Him? Is God asking me to surrender control to Him? If so, in what areas?

**Read:** 2 Corinthians 10:5, NIV

**Reflect:** Is God asking me to "take captive every thought" and replace fearful thoughts with faith-filled ones? What are some practical ways I can do this?

# CHAPTER TEN

# TENSILE STRENGTH TRAINING

*Letting Your Children Make You Strong*

*Like arrows in the hand of a warrior, so are the children of one's youth.*

PSALM 127:4

WHEN OUR FIRST CHILD WAS BORN, Eric and I felt like we'd been run over by a bus. Hudson was an extremely high-maintenance baby, and he hardly ever slept. Other children seemed to sleep serenely in their strollers while their parents walked peacefully through the mall or the park. Hudson was wired for sound, wide-awake, fidgeting, fussing, and wanting attention almost twenty-four hours a day. Other moms would brag about how their newborns slept for eight hours each night from the day they came home from the hospital. Hudson had acid reflux, which caused him to wake up screaming every thirty or forty minutes all night long. After about four months of this, I was at my wit's end. We hadn't gotten more than a couple hours of sleep each night since he'd arrived. We were trying to fulfill book deadlines and run our ministry, but we were so worn down from the new adventure of parenting that we could hardly function.

Though we loved our little boy, we wondered what God had been thinking when He sent such a high-needs baby our way. The Bible says that children will bring strength into their parents' lives (see Ps. 127:4-5). But having a child only seemed to fill our lives with exhaustion. Parenthood certainly wasn't making us strong. Or was it?

Several months into our new life of fatigue and sleeplessness, God began to awaken us to a hidden opportunity being presented to us through our baby: the opportunity for tensile strength training. "Tensile strength" refers to the maximum stress a material can take under tension. For example, a rope's tensile strength is measured by tying weights to the rope and then dropping the rope to see how much weight it can endure without breaking. The greater the ability of the rope to endure weight and combative force, the stronger the tensile rating.

The strength of our souls can be measured in a similar way. If we have never built our tensile strength, then even the smallest weights and stresses can cause us to snap. But if we train like an Olympian to build our tensile strength, our souls will be able to endure weights as gargantuan as imprisonment and torture. The heroic Christians throughout history who gave up their lives for Christ trained their souls to handle the greatest pressures and stresses life could throw their way.

It was no accident that Eric and I were being tested in this area through our son Hudson. As I mentioned earlier, we named him after Hudson Taylor, the great missionary to China, because we admired this man's example of courage and strength in the midst of great difficulties. Throughout his life on the mission field amid diseases, poverty, personal loss, and persecution, Hudson Taylor faced incredible hardship beyond what a normal human can handle. Most others would have crumbled physically and emotionally under the weights that he carried in taking the gospel to a hostile land, facing the death of loved ones, and being hit with terrible sicknesses. But by God's grace, Hudson Taylor allowed each challenge, each trial, and each hardship to build his inner tensile strength. And thus, every difficulty that came into his life only made him stronger. Now, we were being tested in the very principles that hallmarked the life of our son's namesake.

Eric and I realized that the difficulty and inconvenience of raising a high-strung baby could either strengthen us or weaken us. It all depended on how we responded to the opportunity God was putting in front of us. Thus far, we'd only focused on the hardship, the lack of sleep, and the frustration of having a child who never seemed to settle down. But now, we began to thank God for the opportunity to be made strong through the new challenges of parenting. We began to stop complaining and instead rejoiced every time we had to wake up in the middle of the night (which was a lot!).

As we embraced the training opportunity God had given

us, it was amazing to see what happened. Though you would think the lack of sleep would have weakened us, we actually became stronger. We were able to calmly handle things that used to crush us. Our bodies became disciplined. Instead of our desire for rest controlling us, we were able to respond to the call of God in the morning, even from a dead sleep, instead of yielding to the desire to roll over in bed, grumbling and pulling the covers over our heads. We began to catch a glimpse of what Paul meant when he said, "I discipline my body and bring it into subjection, lest, when I have preached to others, I myself should become disqualified" (1 Cor. 9:27).

We have discovered time and time again that children truly can help us build tensile strength. Children are not convenient. Newborn babies are not considerate of their parents' desire for rest, sleep, quiet conversation, or a predictable schedule. There is no "break," no reprieve from the responsibilities of being a parent. It is always there, day after day, night after night. Unlike almost any other challenge, young children can provide one of the very best training grounds for spiritual and physical discipline. If we are willing to rise up and accept the challenge, our kids can make us strong and fit for the battles we are called to fight in this Christian life.

God has used the most extreme challenges Eric and I have faced as tools to equip us for the epic life-or-death battles we've had to fight in our ministry.

I shared earlier that when Harper came home from Korea, she remained on the opposite time zone from us, so she slept all day and was wide-awake all night. Right as she fell asleep,

Hudson was waking up for the day. This went on for many weeks, and it felt like many years. So once again we had a tensile strength training opportunity to embrace. And through it, God made us stronger and prepared us for the powerful all-night prayer sessions He was calling us to.

A couple of years later, having two newborns within seven months of each other trained Eric and me how to be ready at any time of day or night to enter into a time of intensive prayer. Our minds and bodies were stretched at every 1 a.m. diaper change and 3 a.m. feeding. We learned to pop awake with a good attitude and rejoice in the opportunity to care for our little ones. We learned that we could survive, and even thrive, on far less sleep than we had always assumed we needed. This reality has brought even greater discipline and power into our prayer life. When we need to wake up at 4 a.m. in order to seek God in prayer, it doesn't feel like an impossible job because we were groomed and made ready for the task through the nightly needs of two helpless babies.

In countless ways, our children have become like arrows in our hands. They have strengthened our inner beings and dealt with our self-centeredness like nothing else ever could. After four children, we are far more able to face challenges and tests than we ever were when it was just the two of us.

When we launched our discipleship-training ministry, one of the most intensive tasks we've ever undertaken, our four children were all under the age of four, and three were in diapers. Not the most convenient situation! We had a veteran pastoral couple (who'd never had children) tell us that because of the extra responsibility of having so many young children, we would not be able to handle all the pressures and responsibilities that come along with a discipleship ministry.

Yet the opposite has been true! Our children trained us to stay spiritually sharp, to say no to laziness and weakness, and to do hard things without complaining or arguing. Without parenting as a training ground, I'm not sure we would have been equipped for the intensity, responsibility, and discipline of the ministry we were called to. Because of what God had taught us through our kids, we were ready for the battle. We have discovered that children really *are* "like arrows in the hand of a warrior" (Ps. 127:4). Though they seem to usher only weakness into a parent's life, in God's pattern they bring the most amazing strength.

## WAKING UP WITH A HEAVENLY ATTITUDE

Have you ever heard that old saying, "If Mama ain't happy, ain't nobody happy!"? I used to laugh at this quirky phrase, but now that I'm a mother, I've found it has a lot of truth to it! My attitude affects the spirit and atmosphere of my home, husband, and children in a dramatic way. If I am tense, stressed out, and frazzled, then the household seems to follow suit. If I am peaceful, joyful, and constant of soul, then our home feels peaceful as well, even if things are a mess and the kids are acting wild.

It all comes down to attitude. Is my attitude right with

God? Is my perspective in alignment with His Truth? Am I joy-fully yielding to each opportunity to grow in tensile strength? If not, I'm in for a long, frustrating, and exhausting day where I unsuccessfully try to be a great wife and mother in my own strength.

But when I align my attitude with the Word of God first thing in the morning, I wake with a song in my heart and the perspective, "This is the day the LORD has made; we will rejoice and be glad in it" (Ps. 118:24). This makes a world of difference in how the rest of the day flows.

At certain times of year it is easier for me to have this perspective than at others. It isn't hard to rise early with a song in my heart when I can hear birds chirping outside my window and the warm light of the sun flooding in. But it's a different story rising in the dead of winter when it's pitch-dark and below zero.

It takes supernatural grace to embrace daily opportuni-ties for building tensile strength. Instead of waking up and consulting my emotions by asking, *How am I feeling right now?* or *What do I want to get out of today?* or *How can I avoid the discomfort of getting out of bed right now?* I have to call on the grace of God to ask a new question first thing in the morning: *Lord, how can I live for Your glory alone today?* It's surprising what God can do when I begin my day with this joyfully surrendered attitude.

One of my greatest inspirations is a woman named Elizabeth Fry, a Quaker who lived several centuries ago. Though she had a husband, numerous children, and an active, comfortable life, she began asking that question every morning upon rising. Soon God led her to a women's prison in her community where the inmates were being treated like animals. She began to visit the prison, bringing food, care, comfort, love, and hope to women who had lost their desire to live. The prison was completely transformed. Elizabeth became a powerful tool in the hand of God to deliver the gospel to the poor and discarded. Women's lives were forever changed. New legislation for prison standards was adopted. And before long, God used Elizabeth to transform the entire prison system in all of Europe. She became one of the most influential Christian women who has ever lived, all from beginning each morning by asking the question, *How can I bring you glory today, Lord Jesus?*[15]

Tomorrow morning when you wake up, try something new. Instead of focusing on how you are feeling (for example, tired, groggy, grumpy, unmotivated, cold, and so on), ask, *Lord, how can I live for Your glory alone today?* And then rely upon His supernatural grace to give you a spring in your step and a song in your heart as you surrender to Him, even in the midst of a dark, cold, dreary winter morning or a stressful day when your children seem more needy and whiny than your emotions can handle.

If your children are bringing difficulties and inconveniences into your life (and what kids don't at some level?), I encourage you to see these as opportunities God has given you. Allow Him to use each challenge in your parenting to produce greater tensile strength in your life. You will be delighted at how, in your weakness, He can make you stronger than you ever thought possible—temper tantrums, morning sickness, sleepless nights, little-kid messes, and all!

## LET'S TALK ABOUT IT

*Group Study and Discussion*

1. **Read 1 Thessalonians 5:18.** What is the attitude God asks us to have toward every situation we face in life, including challenges in our parenting?
2. **Read James 1:2.** How can parenting challenges strengthen us spiritually? What is required in order for us to benefit from the various trials God brings into our lives?
3. **Read Psalm 127:4.** What are some specific ways your children have made you stronger?

## TAKE IT DEEPER

*Personal Study and Reflection*

**Read:** Philippians 4:4

**Reflect:** Am I obeying God's command to "rejoice in the Lord always"? Are there specific challenges I'm facing that God is asking me to approach with a better attitude? Am I willing to ask Him for the grace to do so?

**Read:** Proverbs 31:10

**Reflect:** The meaning of *virtuous* in this verse is "valiant, mighty, and strong." Do I believe that God can build me into a strong and valiant woman? Am I willing to let Him use my parenting struggles to make me strong?

**Read:** Philippians 2:14

**Reflect:** Are there areas in my mothering where I have been complaining or arguing with God? If so, am I willing to repent of the sin of complaining and ask God for the grace to change these patterns?

# CHAPTER ELEVEN

# RAISING LITTLE HEROES

*Training Your Children in Honorable Behavior*

꧁ ꧂

*A gracious woman retains honor.*
PROVERBS 11:16

ONE MORNING when Harper was about four, we were all eating breakfast when she asked, "Can I kiss Hudson on the lips?" Her expression filled with childlike innocence. (After all, if Mommy and Daddy can give a quick kiss on the lips, why couldn't she kiss Hudson that way?)

Hudson, who was six, looked up from his food and thought about it for a minute. Then, he turned to Harper and said in a firm, somewhat patronizing tone, "Save it for your husband, Harper!" and went back to eating his toast.

It was a hilarious moment that I will forever wish we had on film. Though Hudson was not tender or sensitive in his approach, we caught a glimpse of the "protector of purity" that we are training him to become in his sister's life. He didn't know anything about sexuality or purity. However, even at age six he had already picked up that certain things are meant to be kept sacred for marriage.

"I know you want to marry me, Harper," he told her matter-of-factly a few minutes later. "But you can't. You gotta find a different husband."

Hmm. Not exactly the way I would recommend him speaking to the ladies, but still, he's catching a vision for purity and honor. This is encouraging, because as a parent you often wonder how much of your instruction is actually sticking. It's easy to focus on all the areas in which your kids are falling short; all the things you still need to work on in their lives and hearts. But I am finding that when children grow up in an environment that promotes respect and purity, they begin to think and reason from an honorable perspective, even without specific teaching on the subject.

Hudson doesn't always treat Harper as a gentleman should. One moment he's protecting her from rowdy kids on the playground, and the next he's rudely demanding that she share her toys with him. We have a lot more training to do. But it's encouraging to see glimpses of honorable behavior emerging from his life, such as exhorting Harper to save her first real kiss for her future husband. It's given me renewed passion for training up a little hero, one who protects a woman's purity instead of conquering it!

## THE LOST ART OF CHRISTIAN HONOR

In previous generations, it was common for young men to excel in the art of gentlemanly behavior: to stand when a woman entered or exited the room, hold the door open for the ladies, and show gentility and decorum in their language and manners. Young women knew how to speak graciously, show respect to men, and be sweetly attentive to the needs of those around them.

These days, such honorable behavior has all but vanished from our culture. Many of us were never taught much about honor, respect, and chivalry, and as a result, it can be difficult to know how to pass those skills on to our kids.

Before we were married, Eric found a very old book on women's etiquette. He thought I might find it interesting, so he got it for me. As I read through it, I was intrigued. I had always thought of the old-fashioned etiquette rules that were pushed upon the women of the past as being restrictive, uptight, and snooty. But this book made etiquette actually sound beautiful and refreshing. It was all about how a young woman could let her light shine in this world—how she could use her feminine gifts to bless and serve those around her. The etiquette guidelines were certainly far more extensive than anything expected in our modern times, and yet I found myself almost wishing that I could return to a more old-fashioned way of living; a time when people treated each other with dignity and respect; when chivalry and honor were integral parts of society.

While we shouldn't expect our children to emulate the flowery language or stiff manners of the knights and fair maidens of yesteryear, our kids *can* learn to demonstrate honorable behavior that reflects the nature of Christ; boys can learn to protect their sisters, girls can learn the art of serving and hospitality, children can learn to show respect to adults by addressing them as "Mr." or "Mrs.," and so on. With some dedication and consistency on our part, our homes can become places where the lost art of Christian honor is regained.

When our youngest children were both two years old and our oldest were four and six, mealtimes were among the most stressful times of our day. Instead of a peaceful time enjoying each other's company, dinner would be characterized by whines, shrieks, complaints about the food, and sippy cups being launched across the room. Our mealtimes were more reflective of monkeys at feeding time than of civilized humans having dinner, and so we decided it was time for a bit of honor-training in this area.

One evening, we set the table nicely and served dinner in the formal dining room with candles, cloth napkins, and a tablecloth. Never mind that our toddlers were hardly big enough to see over the top of the table or that they kept trying to use their dinner plates as Frisbees. We were determined to use mealtime as a training ground for imparting manners, etiquette, gratefulness, and sensitivity to our kids. We did this for several evenings in a row. It was a lot of extra work to instruct four little children on how to sit quietly, chew with their mouths closed, and keep their elbows off the table. But after a few nights of doing this, dinnertime had changed dramatically. These days, we are still working on mealtime manners with our children, but they are far more aware of proper etiquette and are on their way to becoming little ladies and gentlemen at dinner.

## LETTING ACTIONS SPEAK LOUDER THAN WORDS

In our book *The First 90 Days of Marriage*, Eric and I discuss a common lie many young married couples have fallen prey to—that marriage is the time when you can finally "let it all hang out." There are plenty of jokes about men who burp, tell obnoxious jokes, and pack on the pounds, and women who stop shaving their legs or wearing makeup once the wedding vows are spoken. Sadly, in many marriages this is all too true. Many people assume that once you have "locked in" your spouse's commitment to you, you no longer need to work to win his or her heart, and that you can now be sloppy and careless, throwing all dignity and honor to the wind. This attitude, if cultivated, quickly transfers into the arena of parenting, taking on a mentality that says, *My family doesn't care what I wear or how I act.*

This approach disregards the value of guiding a home, caring for a family, and training up children. It makes home life mundane, unromantic, and yes, dishonorable. It's nearly impossible to raise our children to become little ladies and gentlemen if our own standards for honor are dismally low.

I am finding more and more that with young children, actions speak far louder than words. It's vital that our kids see honor lived out in front of them on a day-to-day basis. I cannot call them to a high standard in their little lives if that same standard is not being honored in my own life. It would be difficult, if not impossible, to teach them to not yell at their siblings if I myself was constantly losing my temper and yelling at them. It would be hard to teach them how to live a disciplined, orderly life if my own habits were continually sloppy.

When it comes to training their children in honorable behavior, many mothers over-teach and under-model. A well-known quote goes something like this: "Preach the gospel at all times, and if necessary, use words." My words of instruction to my kids should be merely icing on the cake, a reinforcement of what they see me living out every moment of every day. What a high and serious calling this is!

At times I've been startled to realize that an impatient tone of voice I used toward my husband or kids was being parroted back to me by my four-year-old. Kids watch everything. They hear everything. And they mimic everything— the good, the bad, and the ugly!

So, it is my desire, by the grace of God, to continually demonstrate honorable behavior, even when I am not using words. Romans 2:21 presents a poignant challenge to every parent: "You, therefore, who teach another, do you not teach yourself?"

Having children has helped me maintain spiritual sharpness. Everything I teach them, I must also teach myself. Everything I expect them to live, I must also live out consistently. So even though it's a little like living in a fishbowl, having those little eyes constantly upon my life is also a great blessing, because it reminds me to live a life "worthy of the calling with which you were called" (Eph. 4:1).

Eric and I have made it a high priority to set the example for our children by building honor into our marriage and home life. How do we do that? We try to speak only words that edify each other. We don't put each other down or joke about each other's faults. We seek to be quick to ask forgiveness for wrongs. We treat each other with respect by listening when the other person is talking, showing interest in what the other person is saying, and looking for ways to encourage each other. We don't "let it all hang out" and allow crudeness into our behavior patterns, even when it's just the two of us alone together. We protect each other's privacy. We take time to look nice for each other. These are all simple habits that, by the grace of God, we've been able to cultivate and model to our children.

Because of the example in our home, our children are jarred whenever they encounter people who are obnoxious, rude, and crude. It's a startling contrast to what they are used to. It feels very wrong to them. And that's how we want it to be.

Of course, we are not perfect in all of these areas all of the time, but we take seriously our responsibility to be role models of honor to our children. As we yield ourselves to the Spirit of God, He enables us to live out His pattern for honor—something we could never accomplish in our own strength.

## TEACHING GENTLEMANLY AND LADYLIKE BEHAVIOR

Children are naturally inclined to spit out their food, scream just to be heard, snatch toys out of their siblings' hands, and interrupt adult conversations. Honorable behavior does not come naturally to them. So, it must not only be modeled but diligently taught.

Eric has a special time with Hudson every week where he teaches him how to become a Christlike gentleman. When Kipling is a little older, he will be joining in these training sessions. As Eric was preparing for this gentleman training, he drafted thirteen principles of gentlemanly honor, which he continually teaches and reinforces to Hudson in creative and practical ways. The list is as follows:

- Always demonstrate honor (no rude behavior).
- Live a clean and orderly life.
- Be an alert and enthusiastic student.
- See what needs to be done, and do it!
- No grumbling, no complaining.
- Protect the little guy and train to defend the weak.
- Don't be a pushover to pain.
- If you make a mistake, make it right—and quick.

*love*

- Always tell the truth.
- Show respect for authority.
- Be extremely generous.
- Eat what is set before you.
- Face the creepy crawlies with confidence (don't be a wimp).

We've told Hudson that when he begins to excel in these behaviors on a consistent basis, he will be ready to join Daddy on ministry trips overseas. He takes his hero training seriously. It's not a list of dos and don'ts he's forced to follow but rather an exciting vision for what God wants him to become.

Harper and I have been going to tea at Nana's house. She gets to wear a pretty dress and learn how to sit properly at the table, show gratitude to Nana for her hospitality, and cultivate the art of gracious, dignified femininity.

We haven't yet developed a specific list of "womanly honor" principles for our girls, but I am working with them on many of the same areas that Eric is training the boys in, such as asking for things politely, showing respect to adults, and being thankful for their food instead of complaining about it. And, of course, there are a few girl-specific things they are learning too, such as how to be ladylike when sitting in a skirt, and how to behave properly around boys their age. (For example, don't try to kiss them on the cheek or sit on their laps!)

All of our children have a time each evening when they

practice sitting still, calmly with their hands in their laps while we read to them, engage them in conversation, listen to an audio book together, or talk about specific truths from God's Word. When one of them begins to slouch, flop, or squirm, we remind him or her, "Sit like a gentleman," or "Sit up like a lady," and they (usually) respond happily and quickly, because they understand what those terms mean.

Gentleman and lady training is a primary focus in the Ludy home. Our children are just beginning to learn these honorable behavior patterns, and sometimes it's daunting to see just how far they have to go on this journey! However, they are catching a clear vision for the men and women of honor God desires to shape them into, and the foundation is being laid.

## TEACHING HONOR FOR THE RIGHT REASONS

It bears repeating: The purpose of instilling honorable behavior into our children is not to impress others with our parenting skills or garner praise for how well our children behave. Rather, it is to train our children in God's ways and to prepare their hearts for the gospel (see Prov. 22:6; Eph. 6:4).

I've known many mothers who dutifully train their children to sit quietly in church and address adults respectfully, yet fail to truly equip their children to know and honor Jesus Christ. Their kids' good behavior has become a trophy of personal pride instead of an outflow of their love for Christ. Their children may act honorably during the early years, but they will likely rebel against their parents' standards later in life. (Eric and I observed this scenario all too often in working with teens during the early years of our ministry.)

When we become more concerned with the opinions of others than with the state of our children's souls, our honor training will go to waste. Children can sense whether their parents' desire for proper behavior flows from selfish motives or loving ones. If we push our kids to act honorably simply to make ourselves look good (for example, "My, what well-mannered children you have!"), they will eventually begin to resent the principles of godly honor that we are attempting to impart to them. But when our motive is to lovingly help shape them into the Christ-honoring men and women God desires them to become, they will be much more responsive to our training, and the principles we are teaching them will last for a lifetime.

Share with your kids the *reasons* for developing honorable behavior patterns, and be sure you don't say things like, "So that you don't disgrace me in public!" or "So that people won't think you are a little rascal!" Rather, remind them that Jesus Christ is honor personified. During His earthly life, He treated women with dignity and respect (see Jn. 8:11); He honored authority (see Jn. 5:19); and He graciously served those around Him (see Jn. 13:14). And when He overtakes our lives, He desires to cultivate those same qualities in us. Explain to your kids that living honorably is a way that we can glorify Jesus Christ, follow in His steps, and reflect His nature to the world around us.

When kids are pointed toward honorable behavior as

an outflow of their relationship with Christ, they will avoid falling into the dangerous traps of stiff legalism or selfish rebellion as they grow older; they will honor God's behavior patterns as an outflow of their love for Jesus Christ. And that's the only kind of honor that lasts.

✳ ✳ ✳

As parents, God asks us to speak of His pattern to our children diligently and continually: "You shall teach them diligently to your children, and shall talk of them when you sit in your house, when you walk by the way, when you lie down, and when you rise up" (Dt. 6:7). It's a big responsibility, but with it comes a big reward: "Train up a child in the way he should go, and when he is old he will not depart from it" (Prov. 22:6).

The world is in desperate need of heroes who will showcase Christ-built heavenly honor. As parents, one of our greatest desires should be for our children to be counted among them.

## LET'S TALK ABOUT IT

*Group Study and Discussion*

1. **Read 1 Corinthians 13.** How does this chapter exemplify the honorable behavior that God wants to instill within our children? Why is modeling these qualities for our children so important?

2. **Read Job 29 and Proverbs 31.** What stands out to you about God's pattern for biblical masculinity

and biblical femininity? How is it different from the masculinity and femininity of our modern culture? How can we acquaint our children with God's pattern in these areas, rather than the world's?

3. **Read Psalm 144:12.** What is the purpose of teaching honorable behavior to our children? How does this prepare them to be the kind of men and women God has called them to be?

## TAKE IT DEEPER

*Personal Study and Reflection*

**Read:** Proverbs 11:16 and 15:1
**Reflect:** Am I exhibiting the honorable behavior that I desire to see cultivated in my children? Are there areas in which God is asking me to replace selfish or sloppy habits with honorable ones?

**Read:** Romans 2:21
**Reflect:** Am I over-teaching and under-modeling honor in my home? If so, in what ways can I begin to "preach the gospel at all times" even without using words? How will this impact my children?

**Read:** 1 John 3:18
**Reflect:** What are some of the honorable behavior patterns I would like to see my children grow in? What are some practical and creative ways I can help them develop these qualities?

# SOME FINAL THOUGHTS

Journalist Sydney J. Harris once said, "The commonest fallacy among women is that simply having children makes one a mother—which is as absurd as believing that having a piano makes one a musician."[16]

What a great reminder. By God's grace I am endeavoring, day by day, to learn the art of set-apart motherhood. Not to just have the piano sitting in my living room, but to learn to play it beautifully, in a way that will bring glory to my King. So that one day, when I stand before my Maker, I will not be ashamed. My greatest desire in motherhood is to one day hear Him say, "Well done, my good and faithful servant."

Remember, the principles of godly motherhood must be approached one day at a time. Don't bite off more than you can chew. Start small. Ask God for the grace, strength, and wisdom to make one change at a time, and wait until one principle is fully established before you try to incorporate another one.

Don't expect to get beyond the frazzle, build your home

into a sanctuary, create a healthy routine for your family, build meaningful relationships with your children, share the gospel with them, and train them in the principles of honor all in one week's time. Simply start on the areas that God burdens your heart with, and lean on His strength and not your own. If you ask Him to establish His pattern for motherhood in your life, He will be faithful to do so.

I also recommend digging into some of the excellent resources that have been written on biblical child training and godly parenting so that you can keep your focus sharp and your parenting on track. Some of my favorites are listed on the following pages.

Additionally, I invite you to visit my website www.setapart motherhood.com for more encouragement, articles, blogs, and resources as you continue your journey of set-apart motherhood.

Well, I need to go see what that crash in the living room was. I hope and pray that this book has brought encouragement and hope to your mother's soul. Know that I am standing with you and cheering you on down the narrow way of the Cross. Remember our God is faithful. Always!

# RECOMMENDED RESOURCES

HERE ARE SOME OF the resources that have helped and encouraged me in my journey toward set-apart motherhood. This is by no means an exhaustive list of the many great resources that exist on motherhood, parenting, child training, homemaking, and family relationship-building. But I feel that these particular resources are a great place to begin, and I hope they will encourage and bless you as they have me.

## BIBLICAL CHILD-TRAINING RESOURCES

*The Shaping of a Christian Family* by Elisabeth Elliot (Nashville, TN: Revell, 2005)

Probably the most inspiring book I've read on parenting! In this beautifully written book, Elisabeth Elliot details her growing-up years and shares the specific things her parents did that nurtured her faith and prepared her for the high calling God had for her life. This book illustrates how faithful, diligent, Christ-centered, sacrificial parenting can turn ordinary children into future world-changers. I have read this more than once and never fail to be inspired by it.

*Raising Your Children for Christ* by Andrew Murray (New Kensington, PA: Whitaker House, 1997)

Andrew Murray is one of the few "classic Christian" writers who really address the practical areas of daily life—such as godly parenting. I have always loved Andrew Murray's writing, and I was thrilled to discover his book on raising kids for Christ. This book is a biblical and inspiring reminder of our sacred, God-given calling to help our children know, honor, and love Jesus Christ.

*Shepherding a Child's Heart* by Tedd Tripp (Wapwallopen, PA: Shepherd Press, 1995)

This book helps parents not merely impart biblical principles to their children but turn their children's hearts to Jesus Christ in a lasting and life-changing way. This book is a practical and solid biblical resource for moms and dads in every stage of parenting.

*Why Can't I Get My Kids to Behave?* by Joey and Carla Link (Bloomington, IN: WestBow Press, 2013)

When it comes to biblical parenting, many books address the "whys," but this book does an excellent job of addressing the "hows." It is loaded with extremely practical principles and solutions for some of the most common behavior issues that children face at each stage of growth and development—an excellent resource for moms!

*Growing Kids God's* Way by Gary and Anne Marie Ezzo (Louisiana, MO: Growing Families International, 2007)

Eric and I went through this training course when we had four children under five years old, with three in diapers. During a season when we were tempted to feel daunted and overwhelmed by the task of parenting so many young children, *Growing Kids God's Way* gave us a fresh and exciting vision for biblical parenting, and we continue to apply many of the principles we learned, even several years later.

## FAMILY RELATIONSHIP-BUILDING

*Creative Family Times* by Allen Hadidian and Will Wilson (Chicago, IL: Moody Publishers, 1989)

This little book is chock-full of practical ideas for training toddlers and preschoolers, building meaningful memories with small children, and turning your little ones' hearts to Christ. I've read it more than once and always find it helpful.

THE BUSY BOOKS series by Trish Kuffner (Minnetonka, MN: Meadowbrook, 1998)

These books are excellent if you are looking for simple, fun activities to do with your young children. They are full of easy, inexpensive projects, crafts, and games to do with your kids using simple materials you usually have around the house. I've turned to these books many times when I'm looking for quick creative ideas, boredom busters, and memory-making activities to do with my kids.

## HONOR-TRAINING

*Teaching True Love to a Sex-at-13 Generation* by Eric and Leslie Ludy (Nashville, TN: W Publishing Group, 2004)

This book is a great tool to help you get started in honor-training with your kids. Eric and I wrote this book before we had children, drawing from our years of training the younger generation in God's pattern for guy/girl relationships. It will help you lay the foundation for honor, purity, and godly relationships even in your children's early years.

*The Princess and the Kiss* by Jennie Bishop (Anderson, IN: Warner Press, 2000)

This is a wonderful children's book that helps pass on a vision for the treasure of purity and God-centered romance. A perfect tool to help your young daughters understand what it means to wait for God's best.

*The Squire and the Scroll* by Jennie Bishop (Anderson, IN: Warner Press, 2004)

An inspiring book for boys about honor, purity, and waiting for God's best. This is a wonderful tool to help plant the seeds for godly relationships even when your boys are very young.

*The Person I Marry* by Gary Bower (Traverse City, MI: Storybook Meadow Publishers, 2008)

A beautifully illustrated children's book that helps young children begin to think honorably toward romance and marriage, long before they reach the marrying age. This is a favorite in the Ludy home, as are the other Bower books for kids.

## PRACTICAL ENCOURAGEMENT FOR MOMS

*Loving the Little Years* by Rachel Jankovic (Moscow, ID: Canon Press, 2010)

This is a great little book that is filled with great tips, ideas, and spiritual principles to encourage and equip moms of young children. The author is honest about the challenges of motherhood, and encourages moms to lean on God's grace to overcome mediocrity and defeat, offering practical solutions for many common struggles.

Mothers of Preschoolers (MOPS)

MOPS is a wonderful ministry for moms of young children, providing monthly meetings for fellowship, support, and encouragement as well as resources to help moms with the many challenges of parenting in the early years. There are more than 3,900 MOPS groups nationwide and around the world. For more information on getting involved, visit www.mops.com.

## HELPFUL HOMEMAKING WEBSITES

EverThineHome.com

Barbara Rainey of Family Life has created a beautiful website and line of products to help women express their faith beautifully in the home. You'll find unique and inspiring resources for keeping Christ at the center of your holiday traditions, as well as memory-making tools that will help bring your family together and build meaningful relationships!

Hannahkeeley.com

This unique website is loaded with inspiration and practical tips for the challenges moms face every day. I first met Hannah while doing a guest interview on her radio show, and I was so blessed by her tireless passion and enthusiasm for motherhood. Her attitude, as illustrated on her website, transforms motherhood from dull and mundane to fun and exciting.

Iheartorganizing.blogspot.com

This is one of my favorite blogs for inexpensive home organization and decorating ideas. Though not from a Christian perspective, it still has many great step-by-step ideas for building your home into a sanctuary of beauty, order, and peace.

# BRING CHRIST INTO THE CENTER OF YOUR MOTHERING.

*set apart*
MOTHERHOOD.com

FOLLOW LESLIE'S BLOG!

My passion is to encourage my fellow moms not to settle for anything less than God's glorious pattern for motherhood. Join me at

**SETAPARTMOTHERHOOD.COM**

where you'll find my blog on Christ-centered mothering, as well as practical and Biblical insights for the daily challenges of motherhood, and fresh inspiration for cultivating Heavenly joy and beauty in your home and family life. Hope to see you there!

*Leslie*

# ENDNOTES

1  Amy Carmichael, *Gold Cord* (Fort Washington, PA: CLC Publications, 1991), 57.

2  Carmichael, 57.

3  Paris Reidhead, "Ten Shekels and a Shirt," *Paris Reidhead Bible Teaching Ministries*, copyright © 2013 Bible Teaching Ministries, Inc., www.paris reidheadbibleteachingministries.org/tenshekels.shtml.

4  Elisabeth Elliot, *Through Gates of Splendor* (Carol Stream, IL: Tyndale House, 1981), 20.

5  Corrie ten Boom, John Sherrill, and Elizabeth Sherrill, *The Hiding Place* (Uhrichsville, OH: Barbour and Company, Inc., 1985), 150.

6  Elisabeth Elliot, *The Shaping of a Christian Family* (Nashville: Thomas Nelson, 1992), xiii, xvi.

7  Elliot, 78.

8  "Six Reasons Young Christians Leave Church," September 28, 2011, *Barna Group*, https://www.barna.org/teens-next-gen-articles/528-six -reasons-young-christians-leave-church.

9  *The Prayer Life* online magazine, http://www.theprayerlife.com/torrey power.html.

10 Hudson J. Taylor, *A Retrospect*, China Inland Mission, London, England.

11 Edith Deen, *Great Women of the Christian Faith* (Uhrichsville, OH: Barbour and Company, 1959), 250.

12 Charles Spurgeon, "Pleading for Prayer," sermon no. 1887, February 21, 1886, http://www.spurgeongems.org/vols31-33/chs1887, 5.

13 Corrie ten Boom, John Sherrill, and Elizabeth Sherrill, *The Hiding Place 35th Anniversary Edition* (Grand Rapids, MI: Chosen Books, 2006), 44.

14 Elisabeth Elliot, *Discipline: the Glad Surrender* (Grand Rapids, MI: Revell, 1982), 101.

15 Edith Deen, 170.

16 http://www.goodreads.com/quotes/22672-the-commonest-fallacy-among -women-is-that-simply-having-children.